HALO®

INITIATION

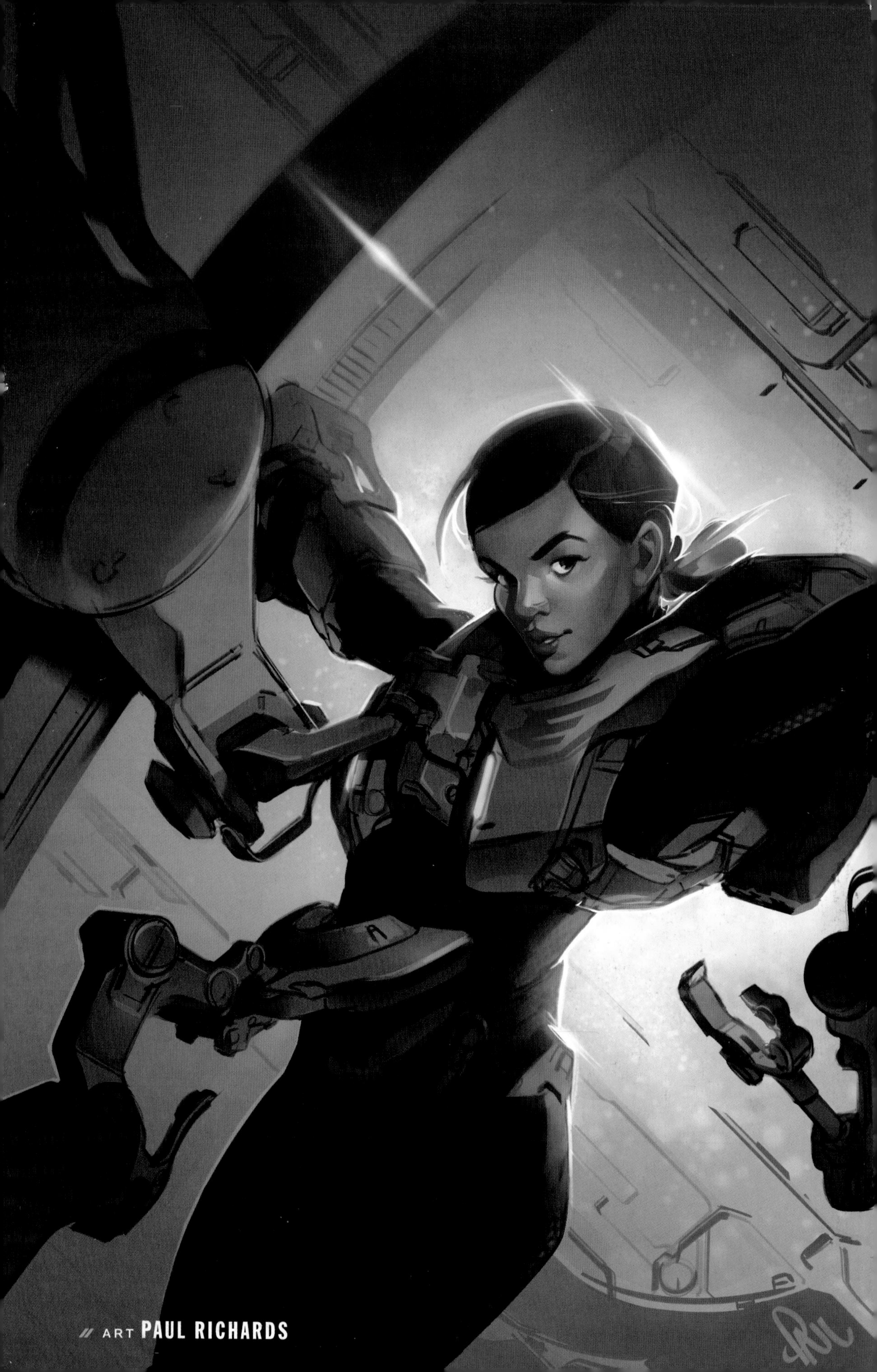

// ART **PAUL RICHARDS**

INITIATION

SCRIPT
BRIAN REED

ART
MARCO CASTIELLO

COLORS
MICHAEL ATIYEH

LETTERING
MICHAEL HEISLER

FRONT COVER ART
KENNETH SCOTT

BACK COVER ART
JOHN LIBERTO

DARK HORSE BOOKS

// PUBLISHER **MIKE RICHARDSON**

// COLLECTION DESIGNER **JUSTIN COUCH**

// ASSISTANT EDITORS **IAN TUCKER** AND **AARON WALKER**

// EDITOR **DAVE MARSHALL**

Special thanks to Michelle Ballantine, Mike Gonzales, Kevin Grace, Tyler Jeffers, Tiffany O'Brien, Frank O'Connor, Jeremy Patenaude, and Christopher Schlerf at Microsoft.

Published by
DARK HORSE BOOKS

A division of
DARK HORSE COMICS, INC.
10956 SE Main Street
Milwaukie, OR 97222

Reed, Brian, 1973- author.
 Halo : Initiation / script, Brian Reed ; art, Marco Castiello ; colors, Michael Atiyeh ; lettering, Michael Heisler ; front cover art, Kenneth Scott ; back cover art, John Liberto. -- First hardcover edition.
   pages cm
"This volume collects issues #1 through #3 of the Dark Horse comic-book series Halo: Initiation."
 ISBN 978-1-61655-325-8
1. Graphic novels. I. Castiello, Marco, illustrator. II. Title.
 PN6728.H344R44 2014
 741.5'973--dc23
                                  2013037372

10 9 8 7 6 5 4 3 2 1
International licensing: (503) 905-2377
First edition: January 2014 // ISBN 978-1-61655-325-8 // DarkHorse.com // HaloWaypoint.com

MIKE RICHARDSON President and Publisher · **NEIL HANKERSON** Executive Vice President · **TOM WEDDLE** Chief Financial Officer · **RANDY STRADLEY** Vice President of Publishing · **MICHAEL MARTENS** Vice President of Book Trade Sales · **ANITA NELSON** Vice President of Business Affairs · **SCOTT ALLIE** Editor in Chief · **MATT PARKINSON** Vice President of Marketing · **DAVID SCROGGY** Vice President of Product Development · **DALE LaFOUNTAIN** Vice President of Information Technology · **DARLENE VOGEL** Senior Director of Print, Design, and Production · **KEN LIZZI** General Counsel · **DAVEY ESTRADA** Editorial Director · **CHRIS WARNER** Senior Books Editor · **DIANA SCHUTZ** Executive Editor · **CARY GRAZZINI** Director of Print and Development · **LIA RIBACCHI** Art Director · **CARA NIECE** Director of Scheduling · **TIM WIESCH** Director of International Licensing · **MARK BERNARDI** Director of Digital Publishing

This volume collects issues #1–#3 of the Dark Horse comic-book series *Halo: Initiation.*

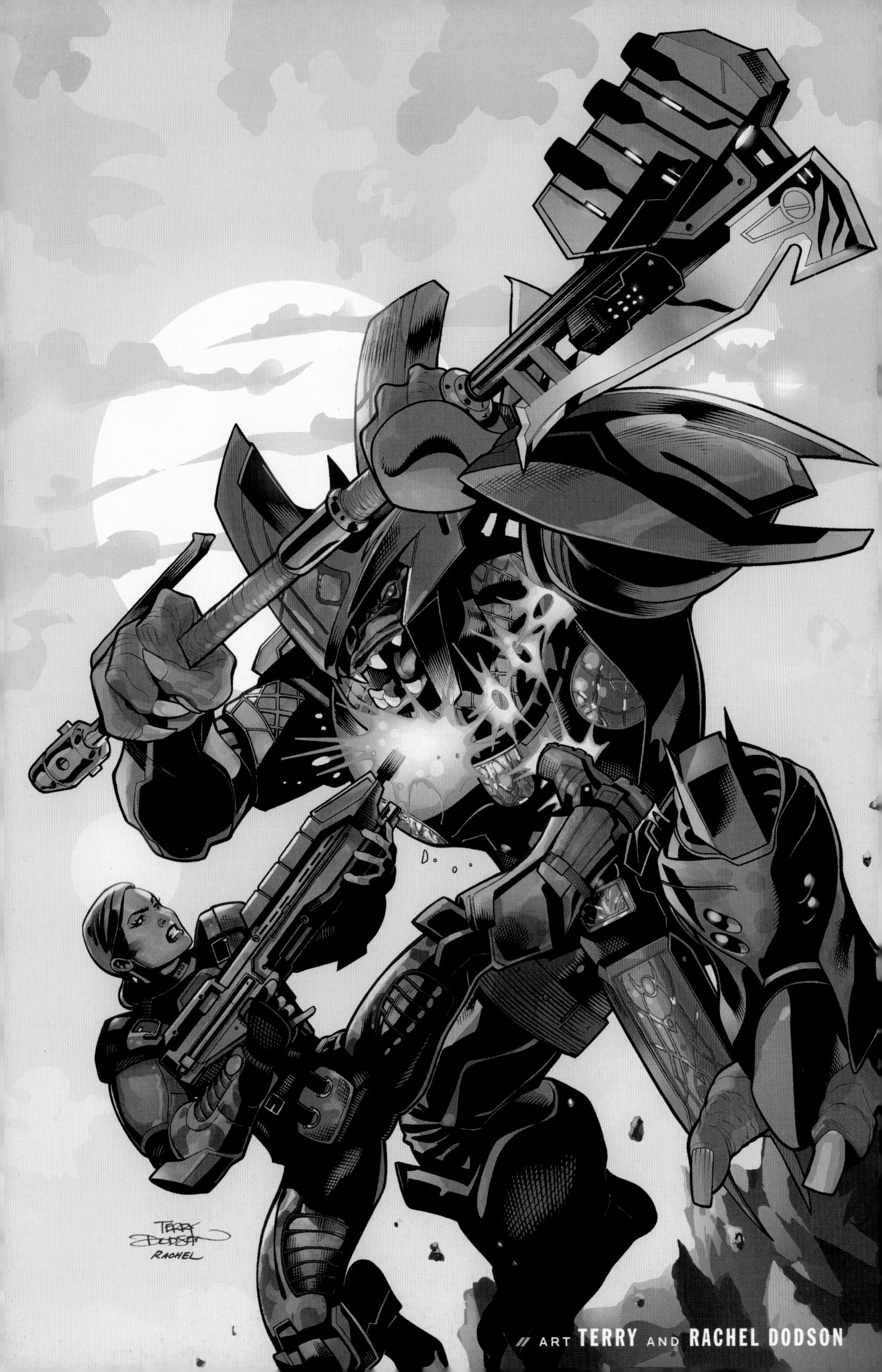
TERRY DODSON RACHEL

// ART TERRY AND RACHEL DODSON

UNSC

UNITED NATIONS SPACE COMMAND

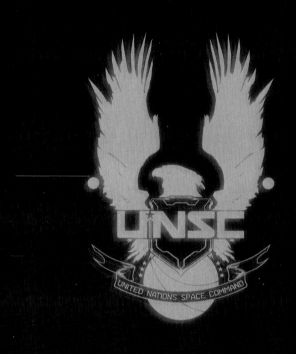

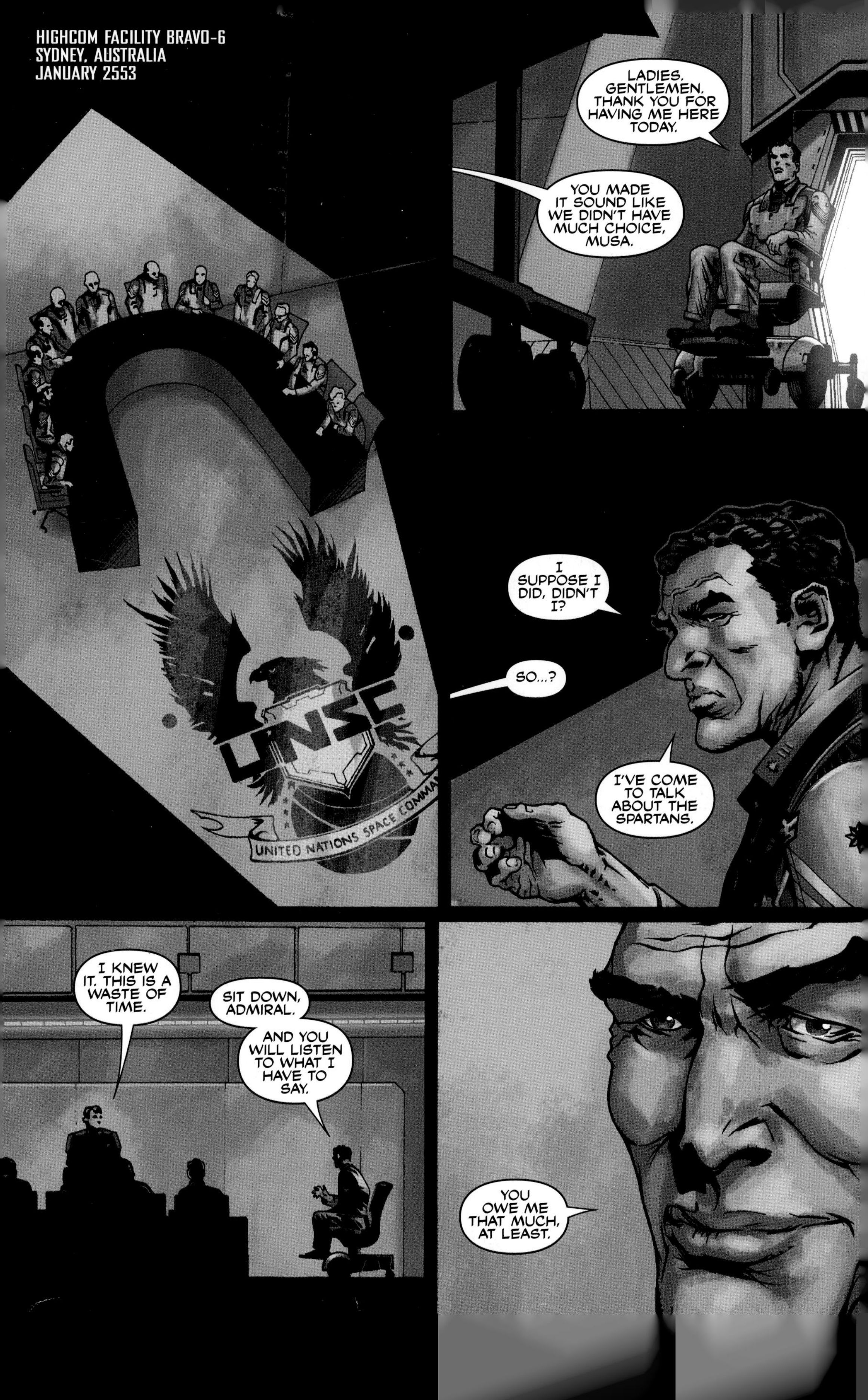
HIGHCOM FACILITY BRAVO-6
SYDNEY, AUSTRALIA
JANUARY 2553
UNITED NATIONS SPACE COMMAND
UNSC
LADIES. GENTLEMEN. THANK YOU FOR HAVING ME HERE TODAY.
YOU MADE IT SOUND LIKE WE DIDN'T HAVE MUCH CHOICE, MUSA.
I SUPPOSE I DID, DIDN'T I?
SO...?
I'VE COME TO TALK ABOUT THE SPARTANS.
I KNEW IT. THIS IS A WASTE OF TIME.
SIT DOWN, ADMIRAL.
AND YOU WILL LISTEN TO WHAT I HAVE TO SAY.
YOU OWE ME THAT MUCH, AT LEAST.

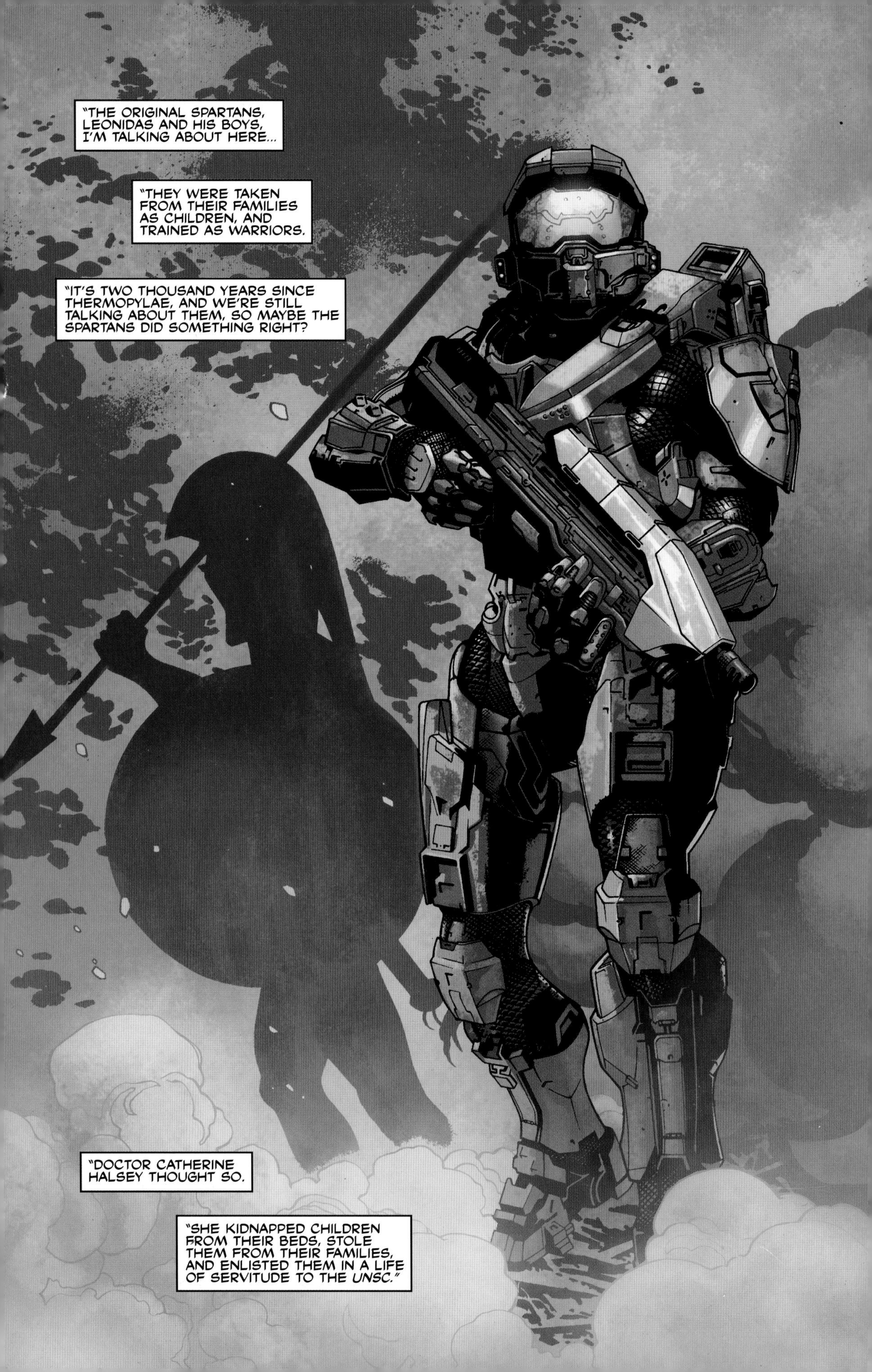
"THE ORIGINAL SPARTANS, LEONIDAS AND HIS BOYS, I'M TALKING ABOUT HERE...
"THEY WERE TAKEN FROM THEIR FAMILIES AS CHILDREN, AND TRAINED AS WARRIORS.
"IT'S TWO THOUSAND YEARS SINCE THERMOPYLAE, AND WE'RE STILL TALKING ABOUT THEM, SO MAYBE THE SPARTANS DID SOMETHING RIGHT?
"DOCTOR CATHERINE HALSEY THOUGHT SO.
"SHE KIDNAPPED CHILDREN FROM THEIR BEDS, STOLE THEM FROM THEIR FAMILIES, AND ENLISTED THEM IN A LIFE OF SERVITUDE TO THE *UNSC*."

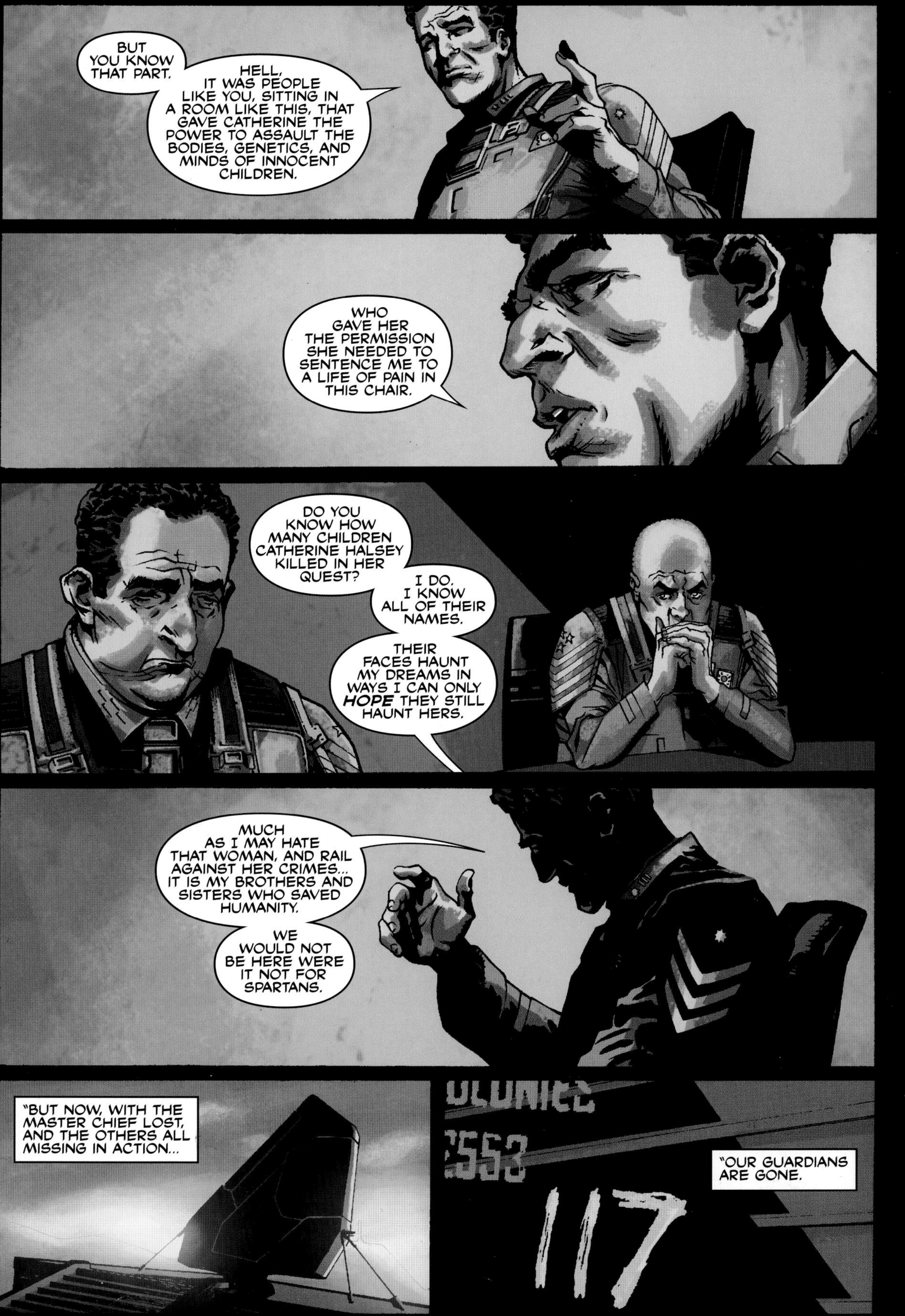
BUT YOU KNOW THAT PART.
HELL, IT WAS PEOPLE LIKE YOU, SITTING IN A ROOM LIKE THIS, THAT GAVE CATHERINE THE POWER TO ASSAULT THE BODIES, GENETICS, AND MINDS OF INNOCENT CHILDREN.
WHO GAVE HER THE PERMISSION SHE NEEDED TO SENTENCE ME TO A LIFE OF PAIN IN THIS CHAIR.
DO YOU KNOW HOW MANY CHILDREN CATHERINE HALSEY KILLED IN HER QUEST?
I DO. I KNOW ALL OF THEIR NAMES.
THEIR FACES HAUNT MY DREAMS IN WAYS I CAN ONLY *HOPE* THEY STILL HAUNT HERS.
MUCH AS I MAY HATE THAT WOMAN, AND RAIL AGAINST HER CRIMES... IT IS MY BROTHERS AND SISTERS WHO SAVED HUMANITY.
WE WOULD NOT BE HERE WERE IT NOT FOR SPARTANS.
"BUT NOW, WITH THE MASTER CHIEF LOST, AND THE OTHERS ALL MISSING IN ACTION...
117
"OUR GUARDIANS ARE GONE.

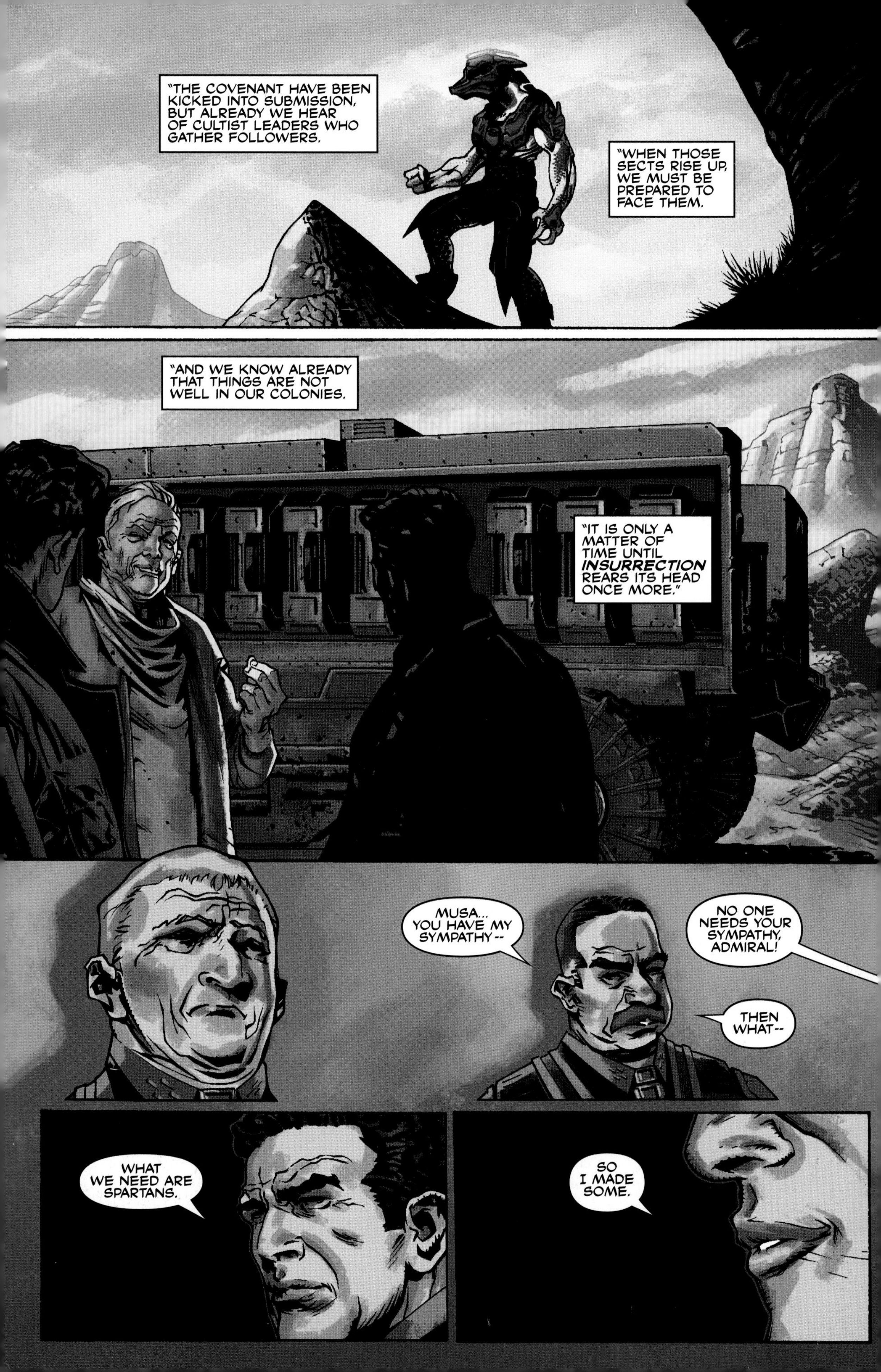
"THE COVENANT HAVE BEEN KICKED INTO SUBMISSION, BUT ALREADY WE HEAR OF CULTIST LEADERS WHO GATHER FOLLOWERS.
"WHEN THOSE SECTS RISE UP, WE MUST BE PREPARED TO FACE THEM.
"AND WE KNOW ALREADY THAT THINGS ARE NOT WELL IN OUR COLONIES.
"IT IS ONLY A MATTER OF TIME UNTIL INSURRECTION REARS ITS HEAD ONCE MORE."
MUSA... YOU HAVE MY SYMPATHY--
NO ONE NEEDS YOUR SYMPATHY, ADMIRAL!
THEN WHAT--
WHAT WE NEED ARE SPARTANS.
SO I MADE SOME.

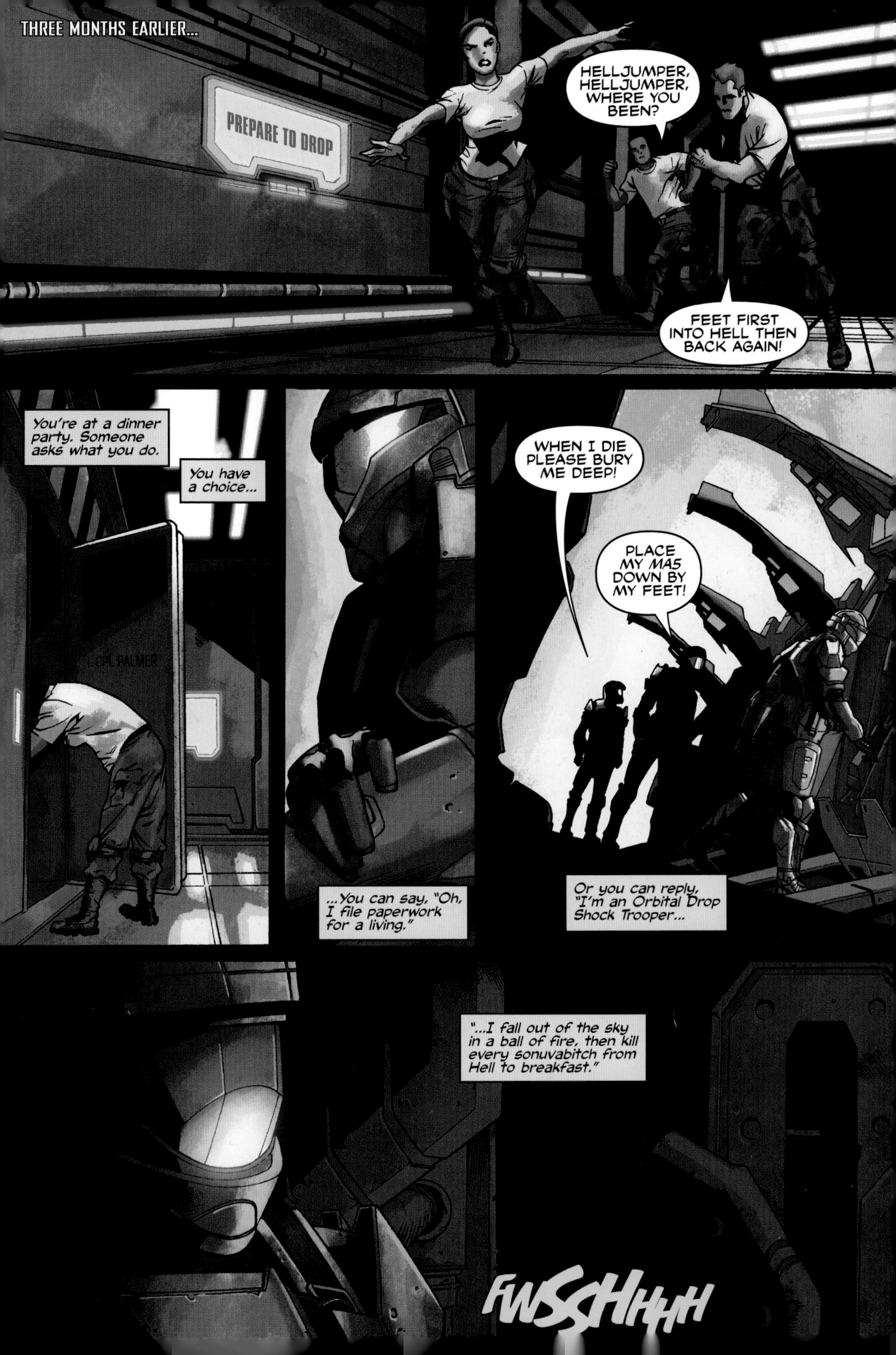

THREE MONTHS EARLIER...
PREPARE TO DROP
HELLJUMPER, HELLJUMPER, WHERE YOU BEEN?
FEET FIRST INTO HELL THEN BACK AGAIN!
You're at a dinner party. Someone asks what you do.
You have a choice...
...You can say, "Oh, I file paperwork for a living."
WHEN I DIE PLEASE BURY ME DEEP!
PLACE MY MA5 DOWN BY MY FEET!
Or you can reply, "I'm an Orbital Drop Shock Trooper...
"...I fall out of the sky in a ball of fire, then kill every sonuvabitch from Hell to breakfast."
FWSSHHHH

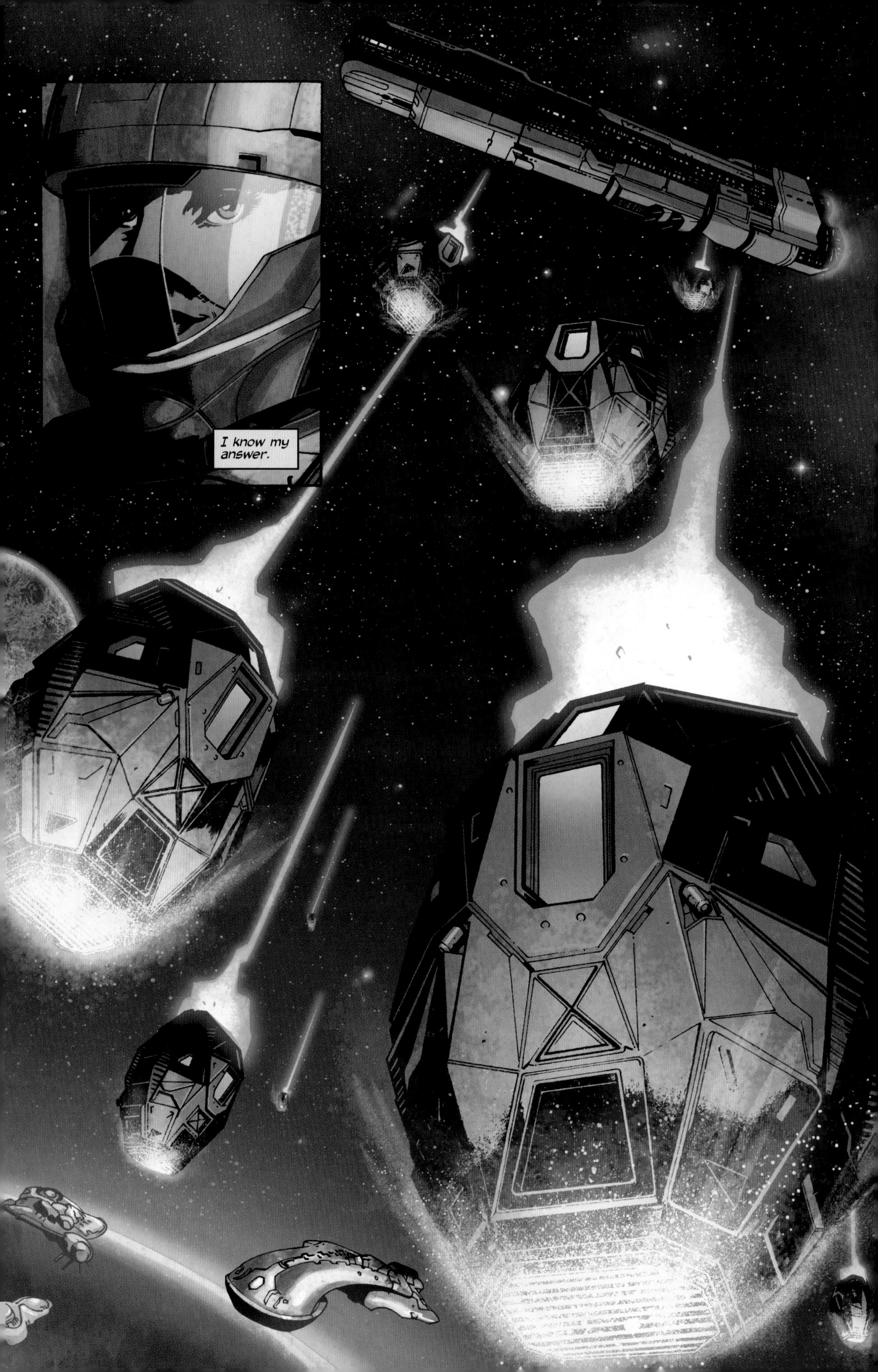
I know my answer.

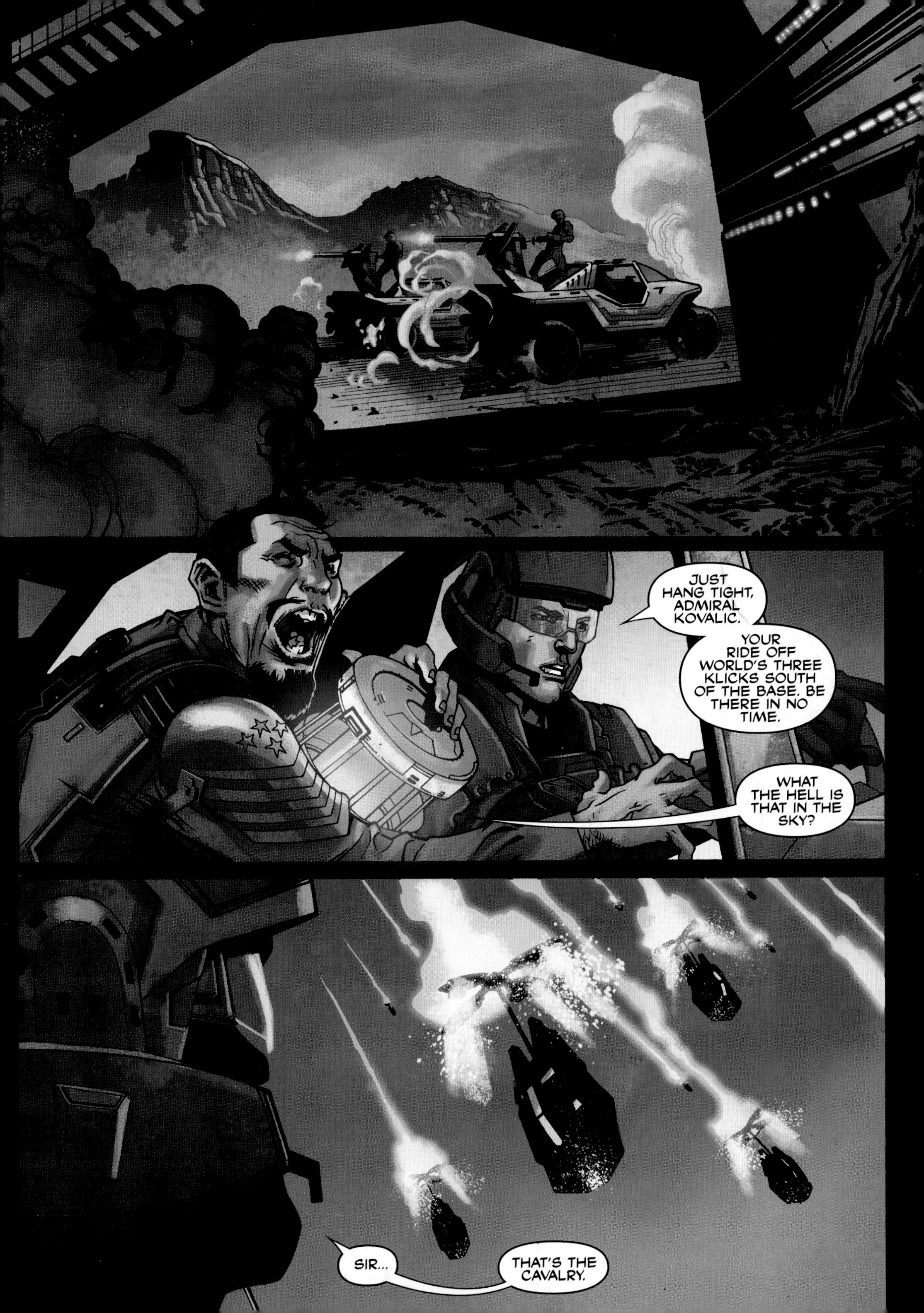
JUST HANG TIGHT, ADMIRAL KOVALIC.
YOUR RIDE OFF WORLD'S THREE KLICKS SOUTH OF THE BASE. BE THERE IN NO TIME.
WHAT THE HELL IS THAT IN THE SKY?
SIR...
THAT'S THE CAVALRY.

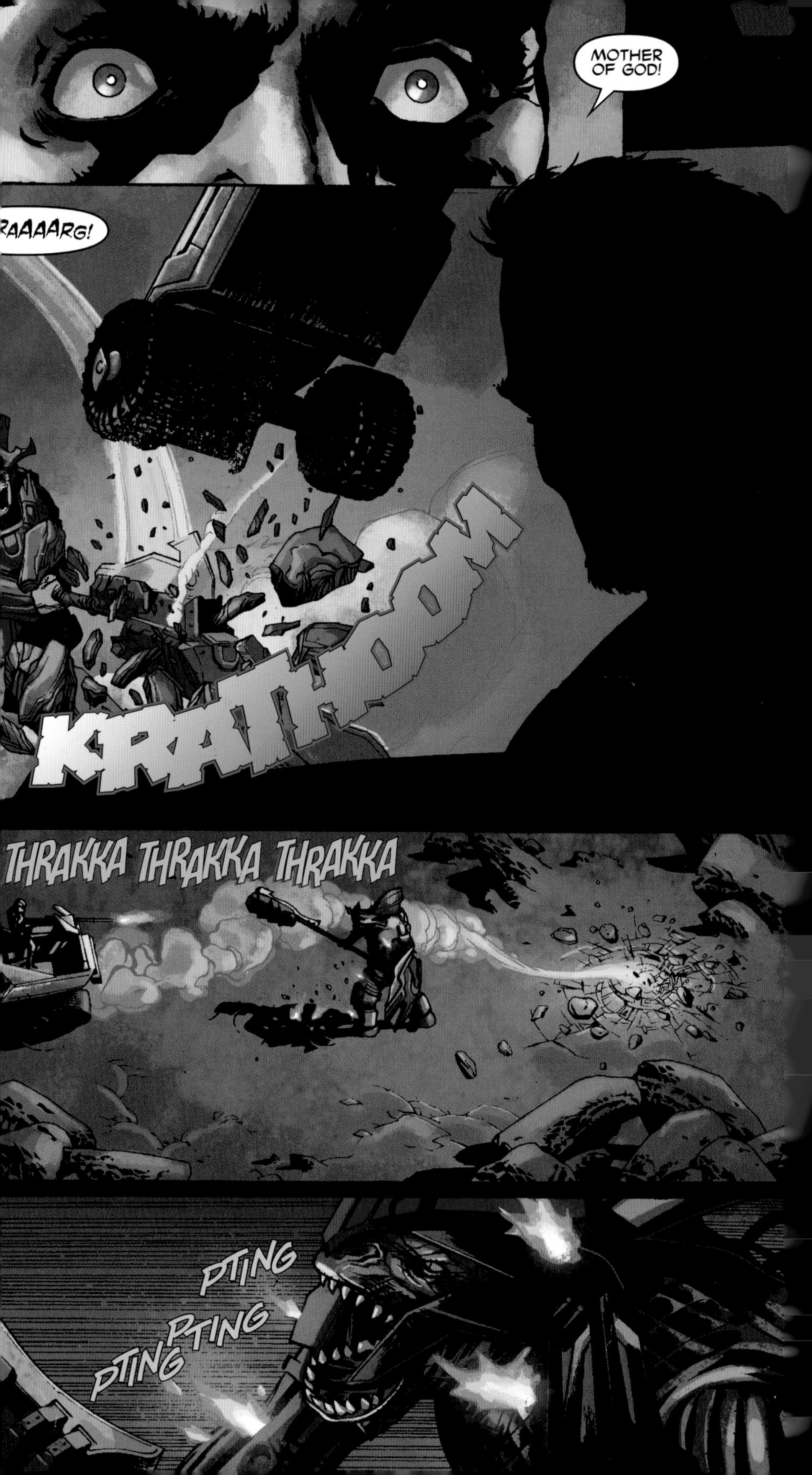
MOTHER OF GOD!
RAAAARG!
KRATHOOM
THRAKKA THRAKKA THRAKKA
PTING
PTING
PTING

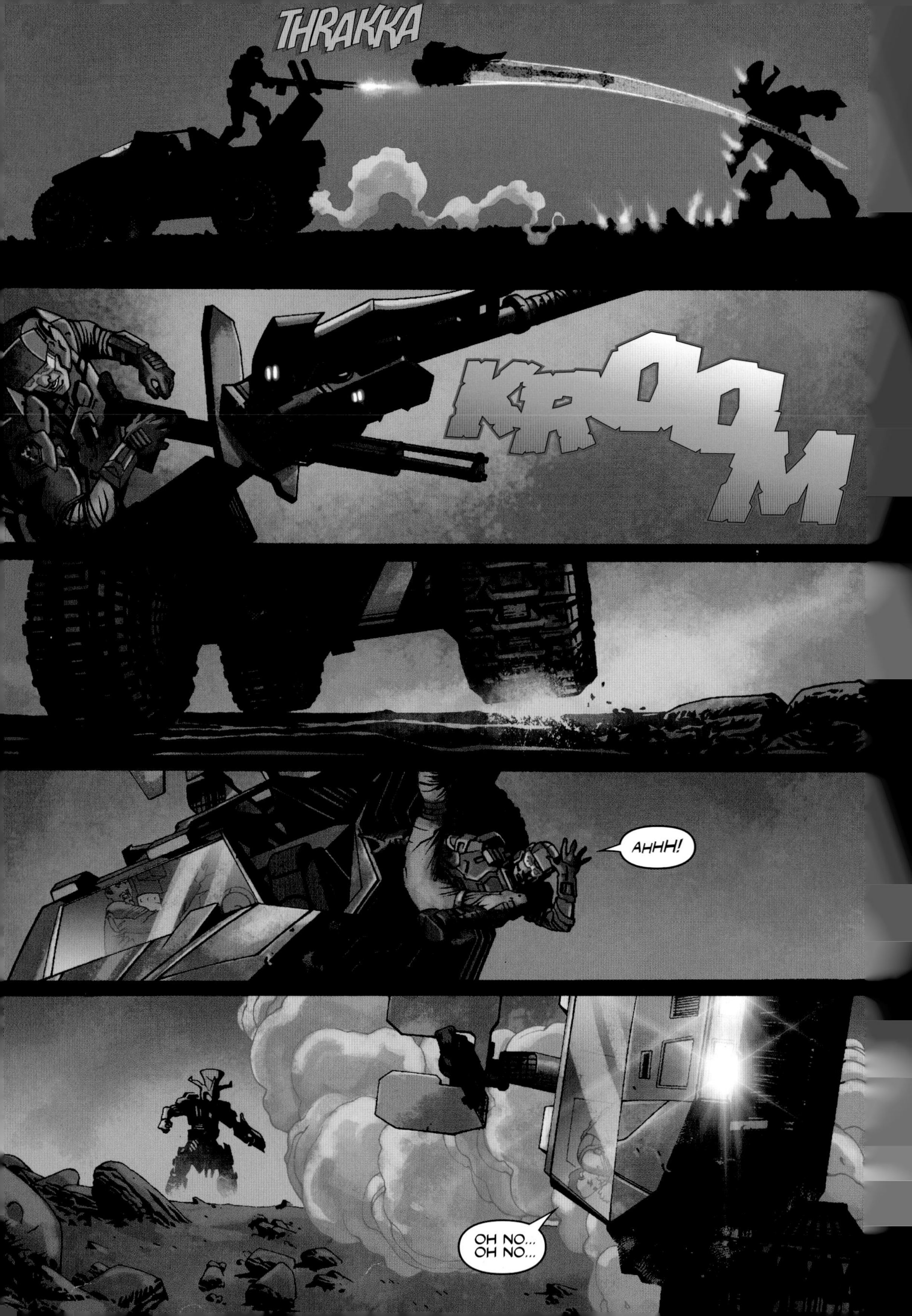
THRAKKA
KROOM
AHHH!
OH NO...
OH NO...

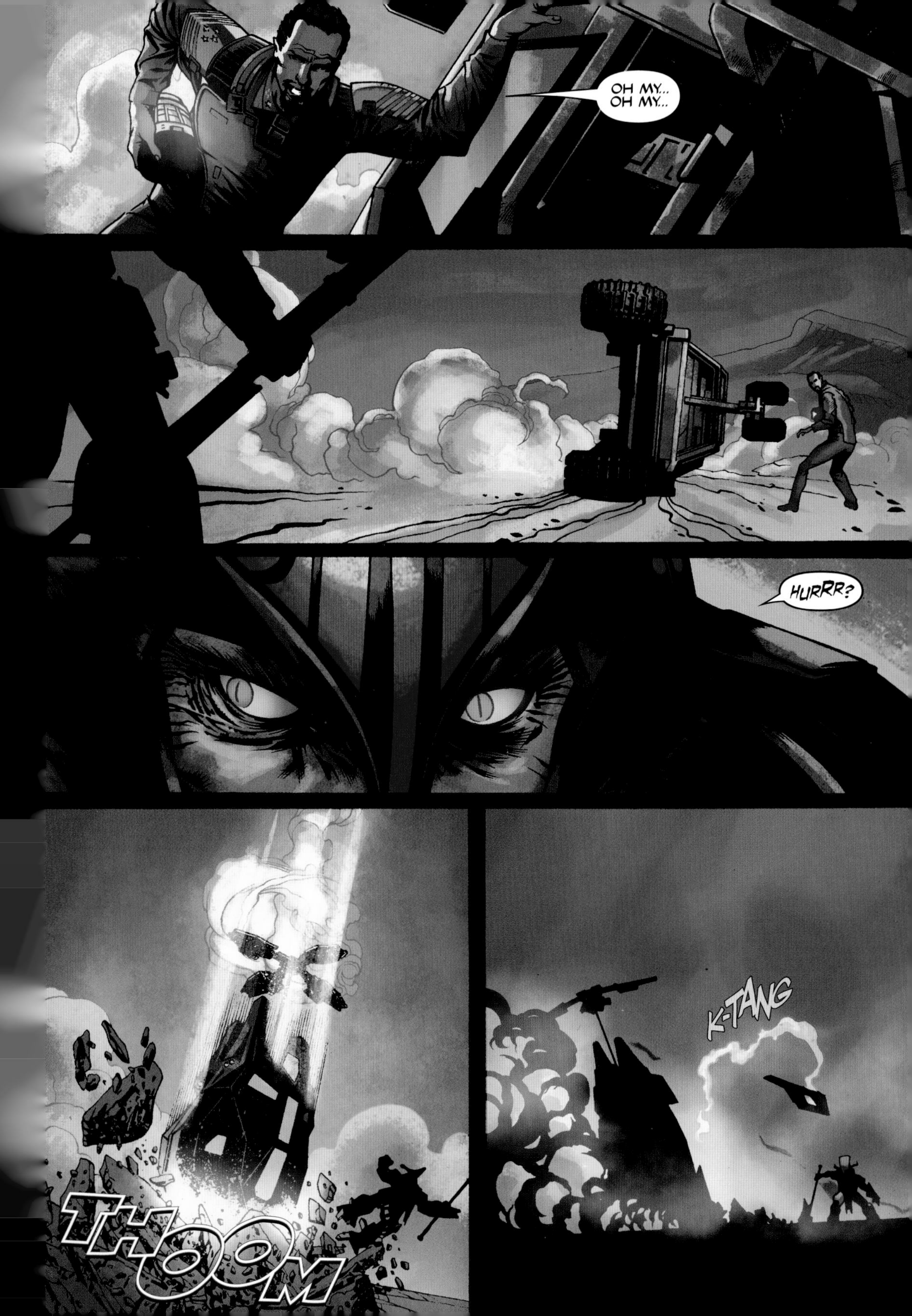
OH MY...
OH MY...
HURRR?
THOOM
K-TANG

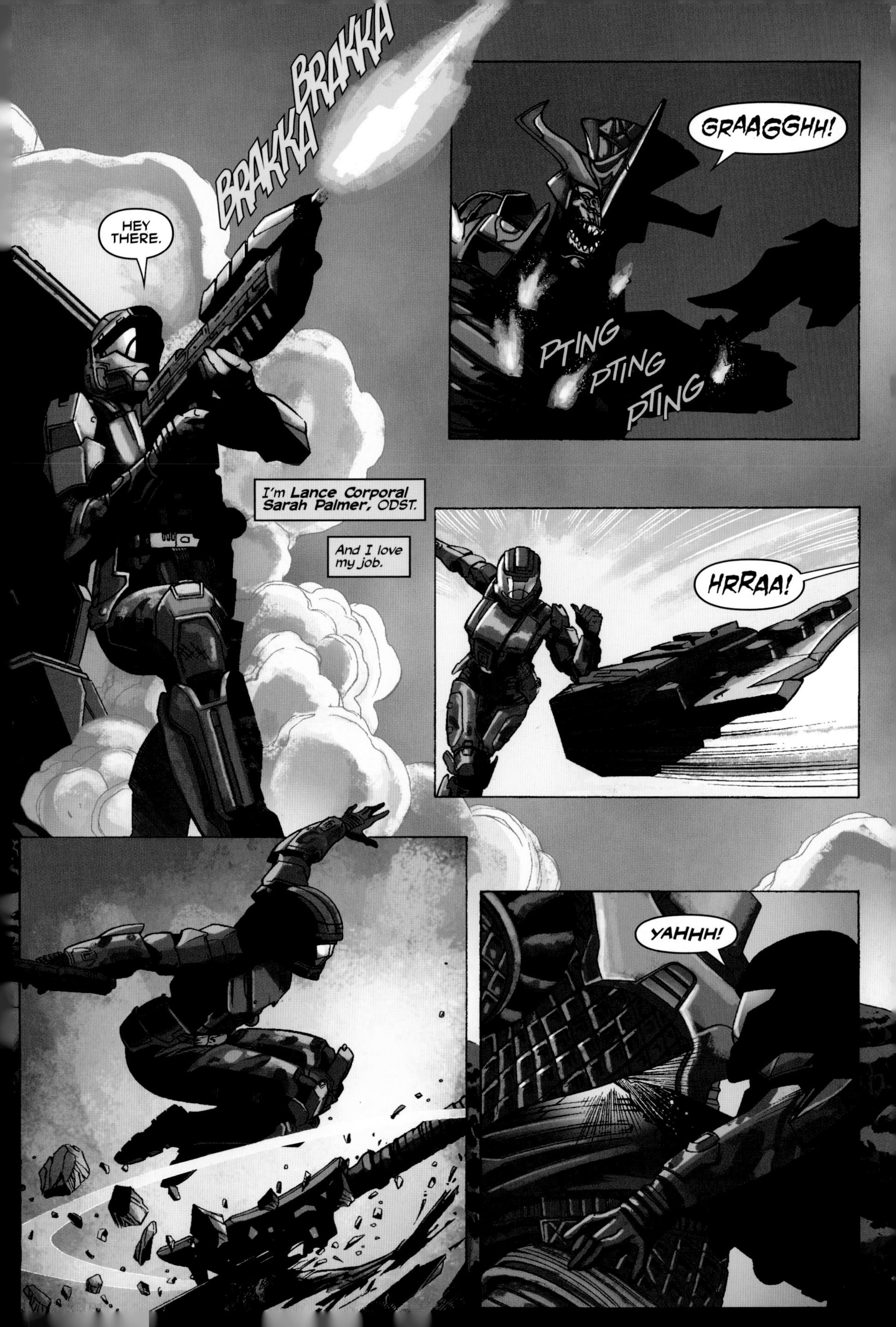
BRAKKA
BRAKKA
HEY THERE.
GRAAGGHH!
PTING
PTING
PTING
I'm Lance Corporal Sarah Palmer, ODST.
And I love my job.
HRRAA!
YAHHH!

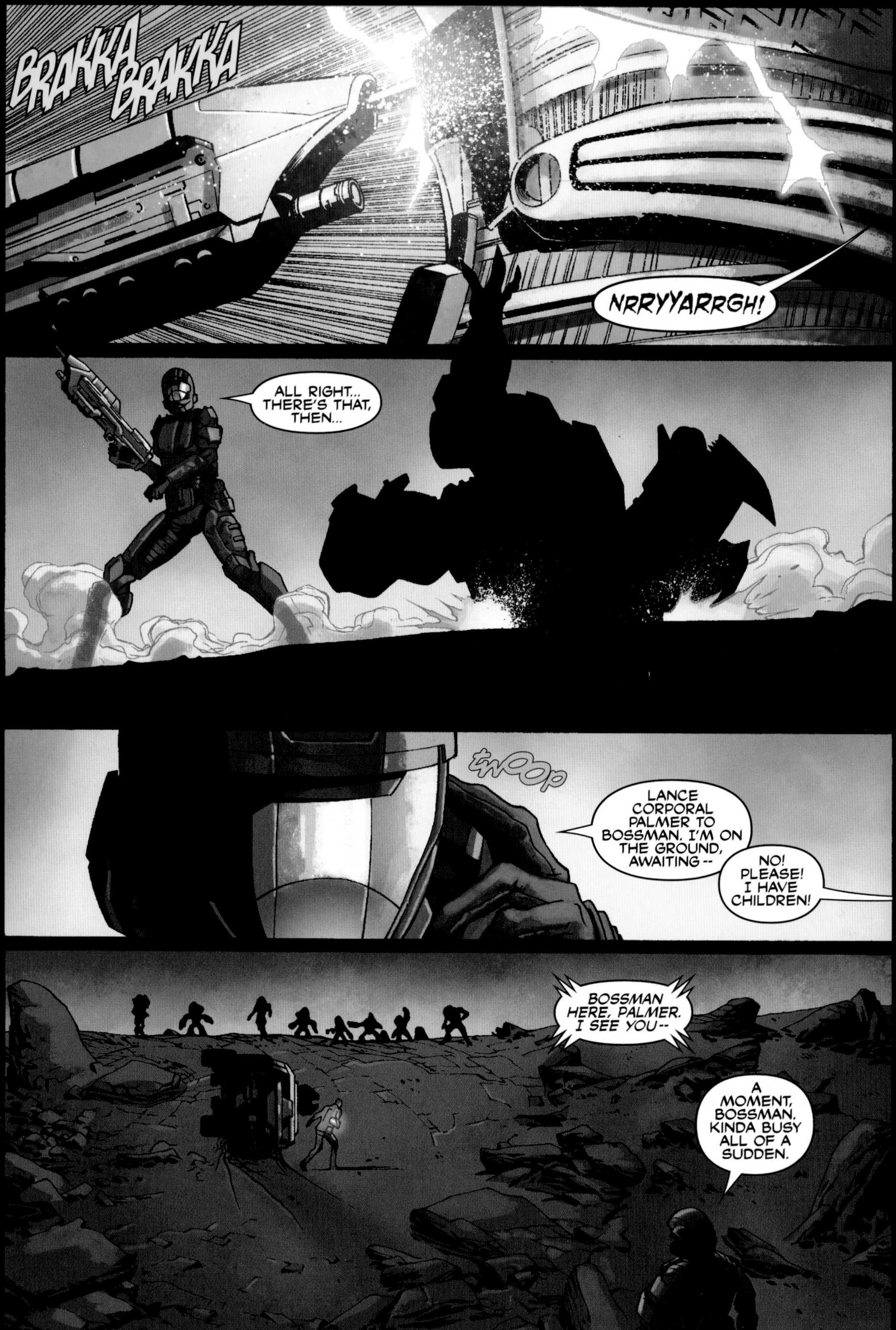
BRAKKA BRAKKA
NRRYYARRGH!
ALL RIGHT... THERE'S THAT, THEN...
twoop
LANCE CORPORAL PALMER TO BOSSMAN. I'M ON THE GROUND, AWAITING --
NO! PLEASE! I HAVE CHILDREN!
BOSSMAN HERE, PALMER. I SEE YOU--
A MOMENT, BOSSMAN. KINDA BUSY ALL OF A SUDDEN.

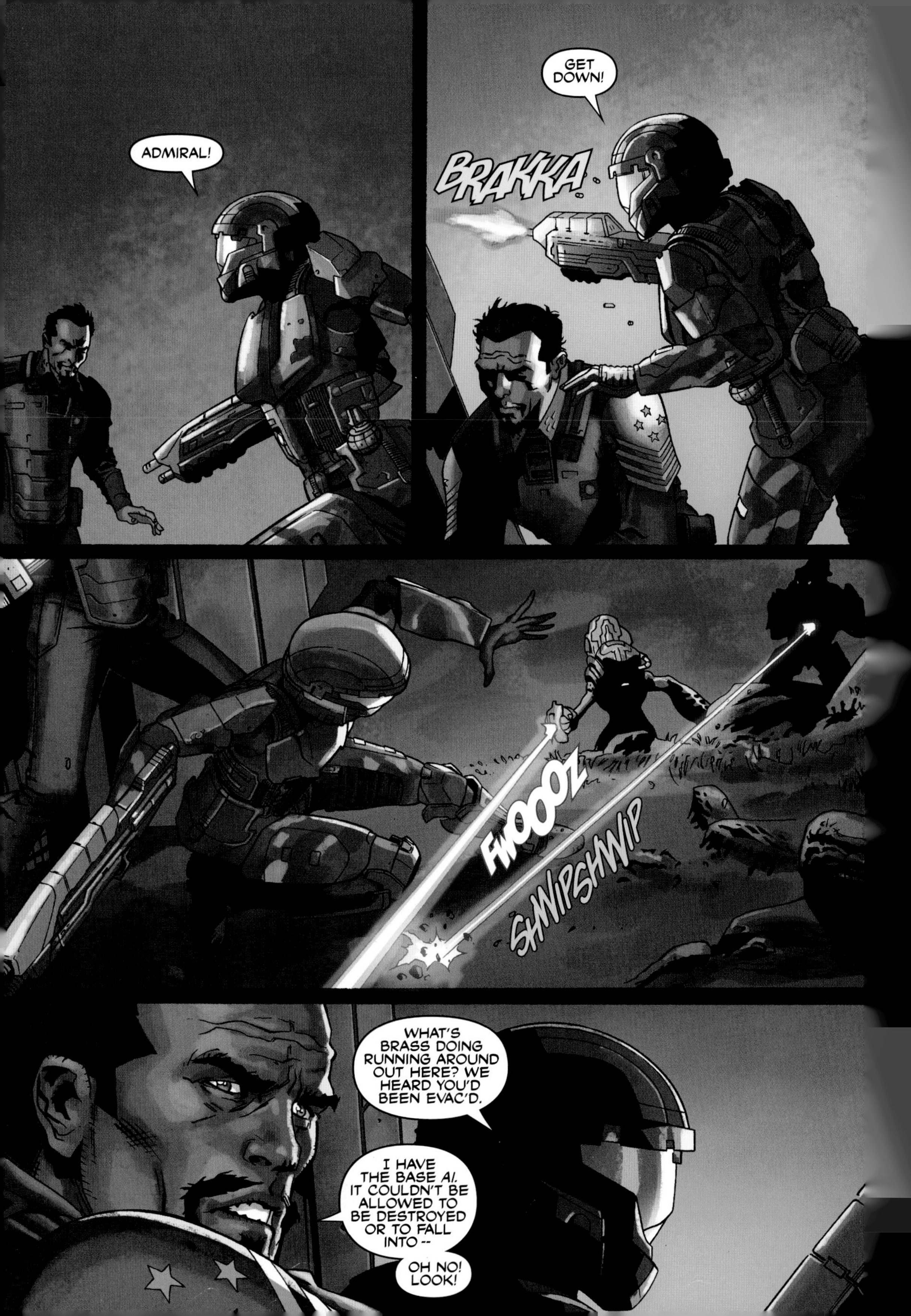
ADMIRAL!
GET DOWN!
BRAKKA
FWOOOZ
SHWIPSHWIP
WHAT'S BRASS DOING RUNNING AROUND OUT HERE? WE HEARD YOU'D BEEN EVAC'D.
I HAVE THE BASE AI. IT COULDN'T BE ALLOWED TO BE DESTROYED OR TO FALL INTO --
OH NO! LOOK!

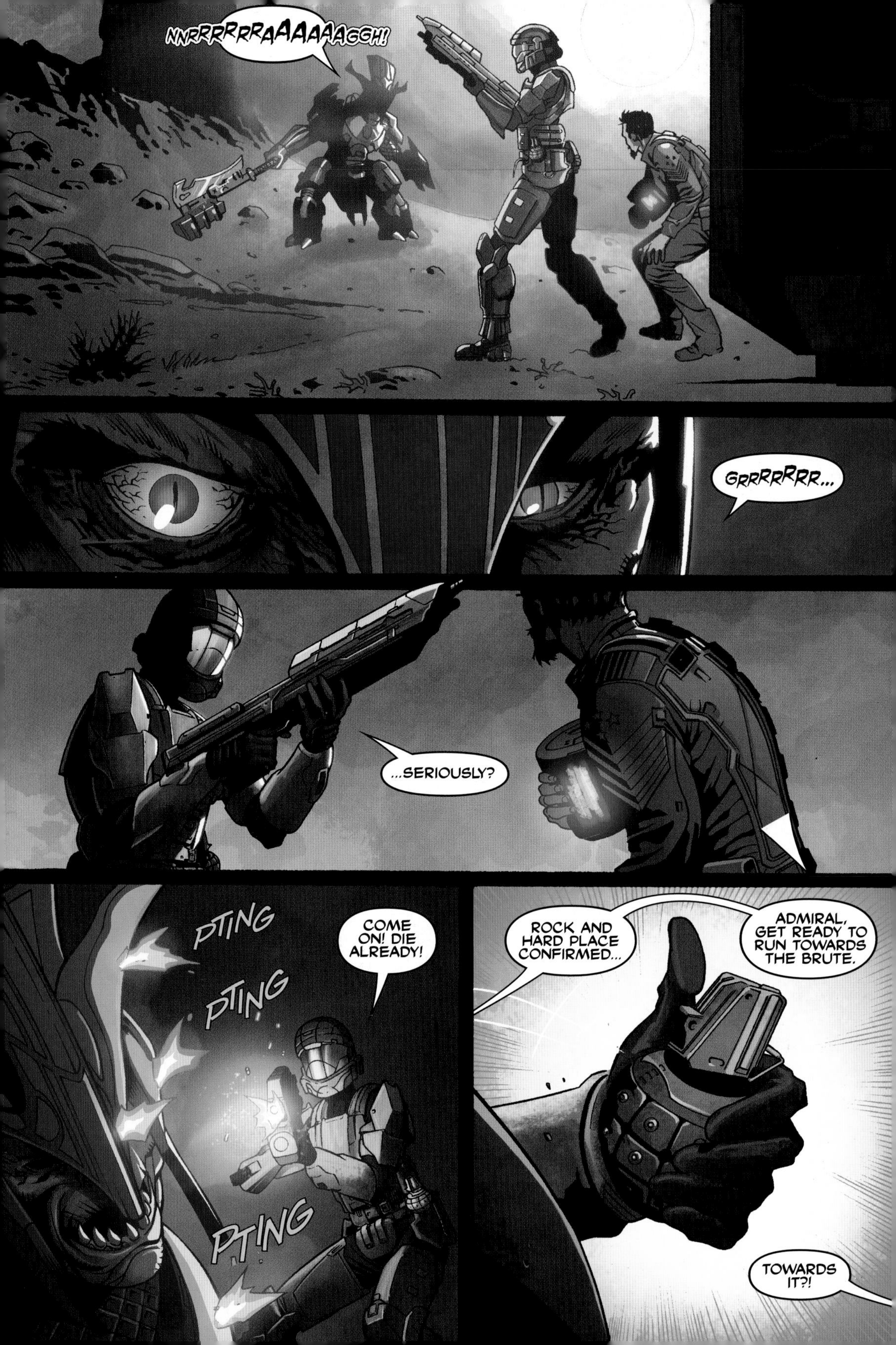
NNRRRRRRRAAAAAAGGH!
GRRRRRRR...
...SERIOUSLY?
PTING
PTING
PTING
COME ON! DIE ALREADY!
ROCK AND HARD PLACE CONFIRMED...
ADMIRAL, GET READY TO RUN TOWARDS THE BRUTE.
TOWARDS IT?!

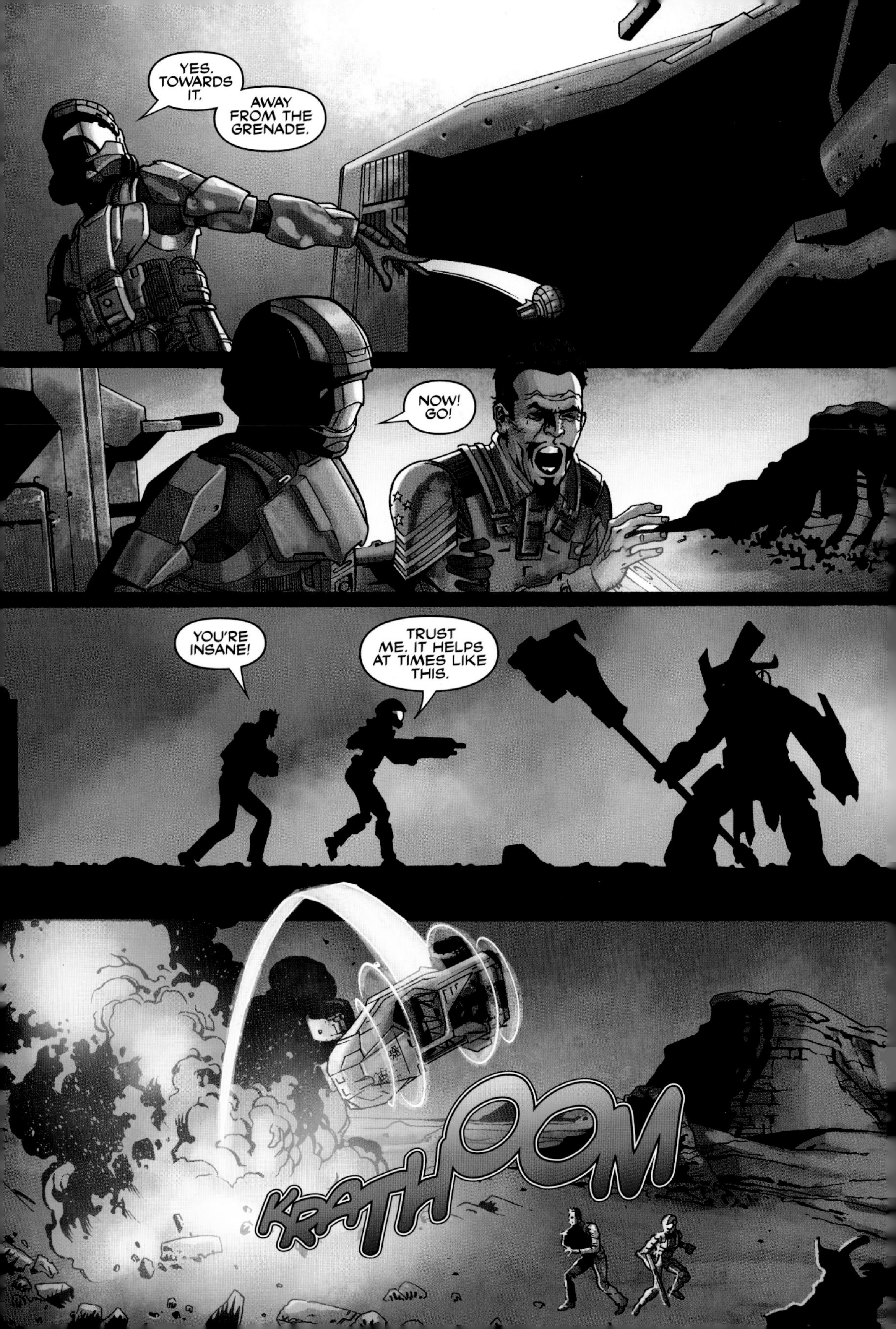
YES. TOWARDS IT.
AWAY FROM THE GRENADE.
NOW! GO!
YOU'RE INSANE!
TRUST ME. IT HELPS AT TIMES LIKE THIS.
KRATHOOM

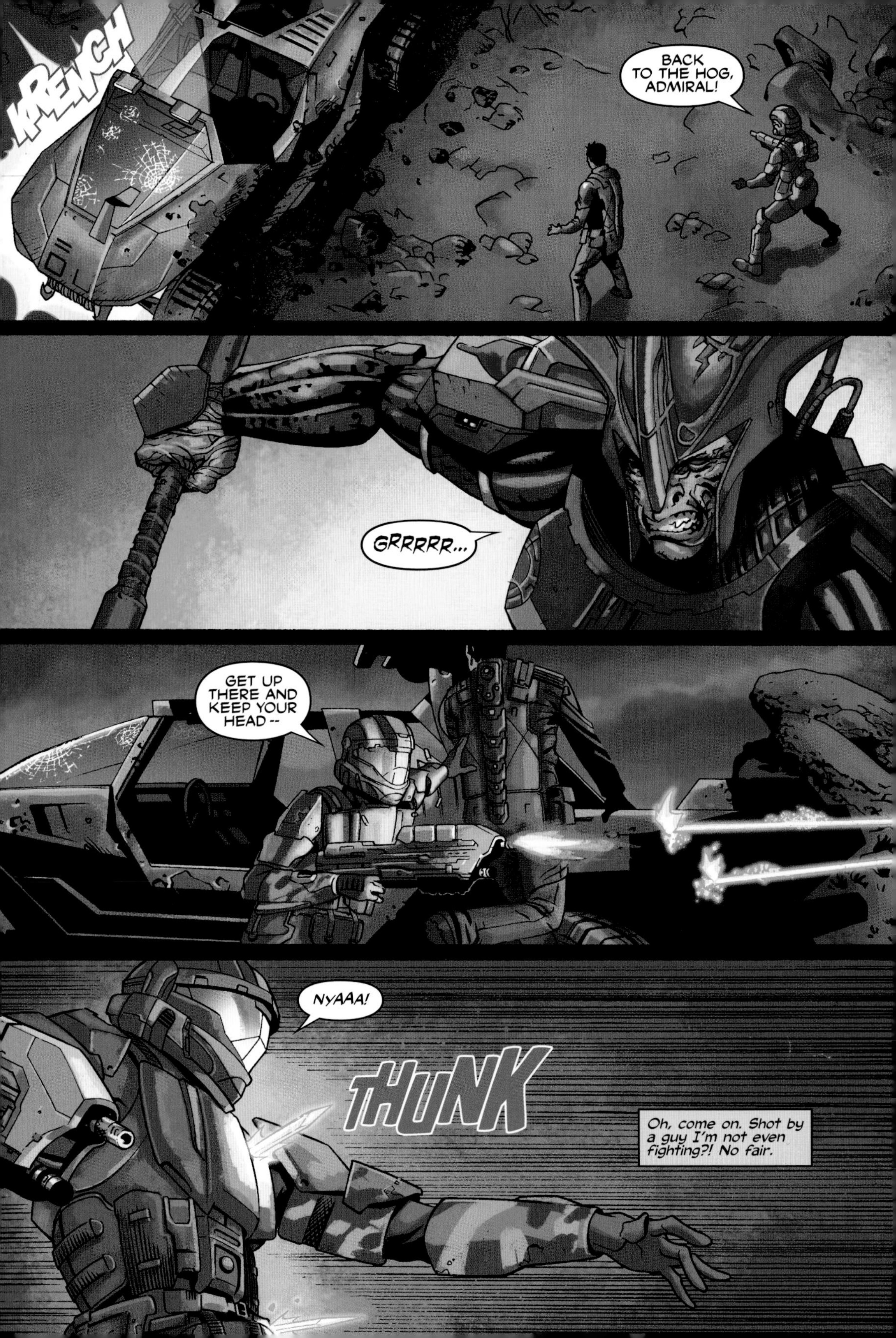
KRENCH
BACK TO THE HOG, ADMIRAL!
GRRRRR...
GET UP THERE AND KEEP YOUR HEAD --
NYAAA!
THUNK
Oh, come on. Shot by a guy I'm not even fighting?! No fair.

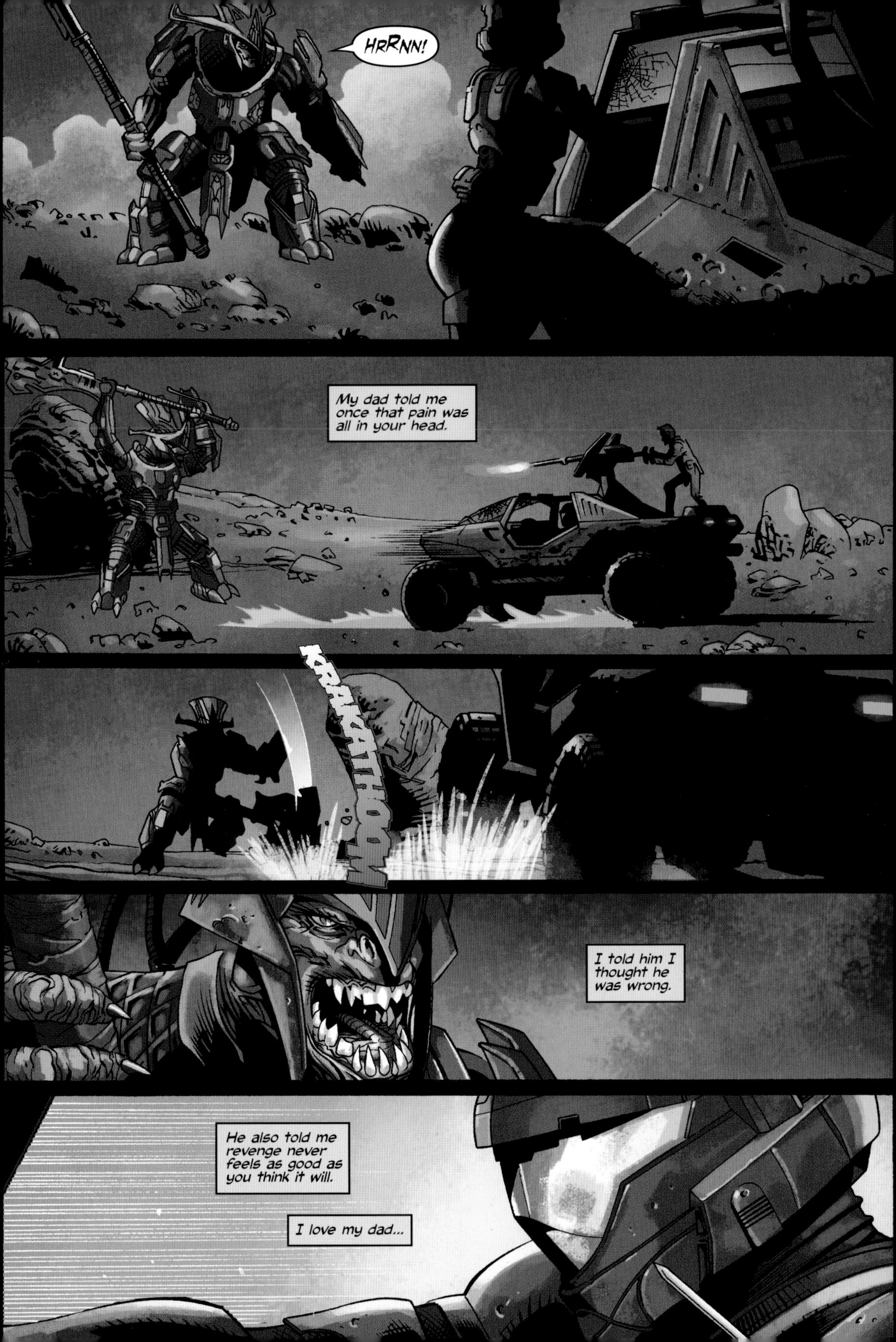
HRRNN!
My dad told me once that pain was all in your head.
KRAKATHOOM
I told him I thought he was wrong.
He also told me revenge never feels as good as you think it will.
I love my dad...

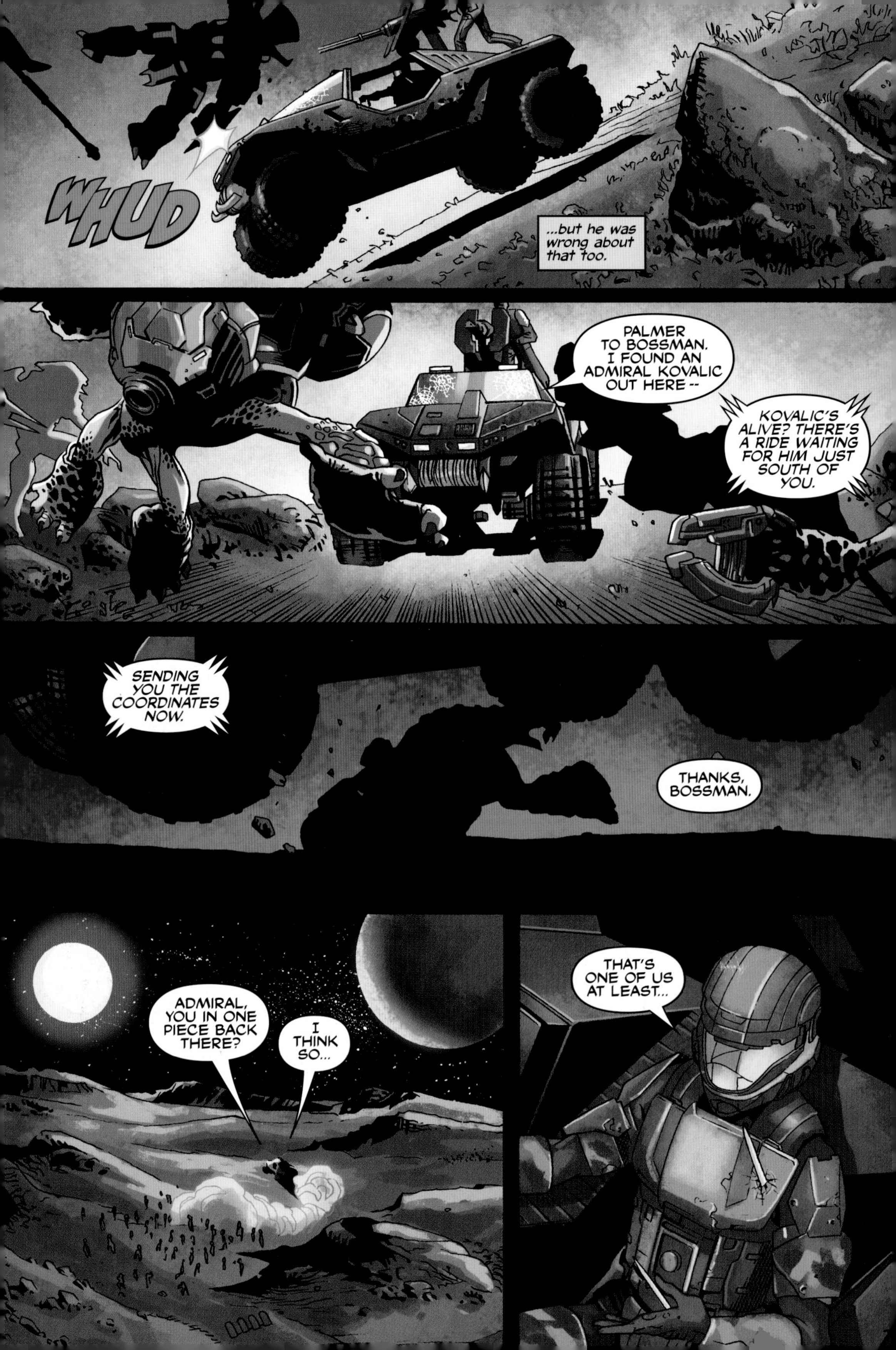
WHUD
...but he was wrong about that too.
PALMER TO BOSSMAN. I FOUND AN ADMIRAL KOVALIC OUT HERE --
KOVALIC'S ALIVE? THERE'S A RIDE WAITING FOR HIM JUST SOUTH OF YOU.
SENDING YOU THE COORDINATES NOW.
THANKS, BOSSMAN.
ADMIRAL, YOU IN ONE PIECE BACK THERE?
I THINK SO...
THAT'S ONE OF US AT LEAST...

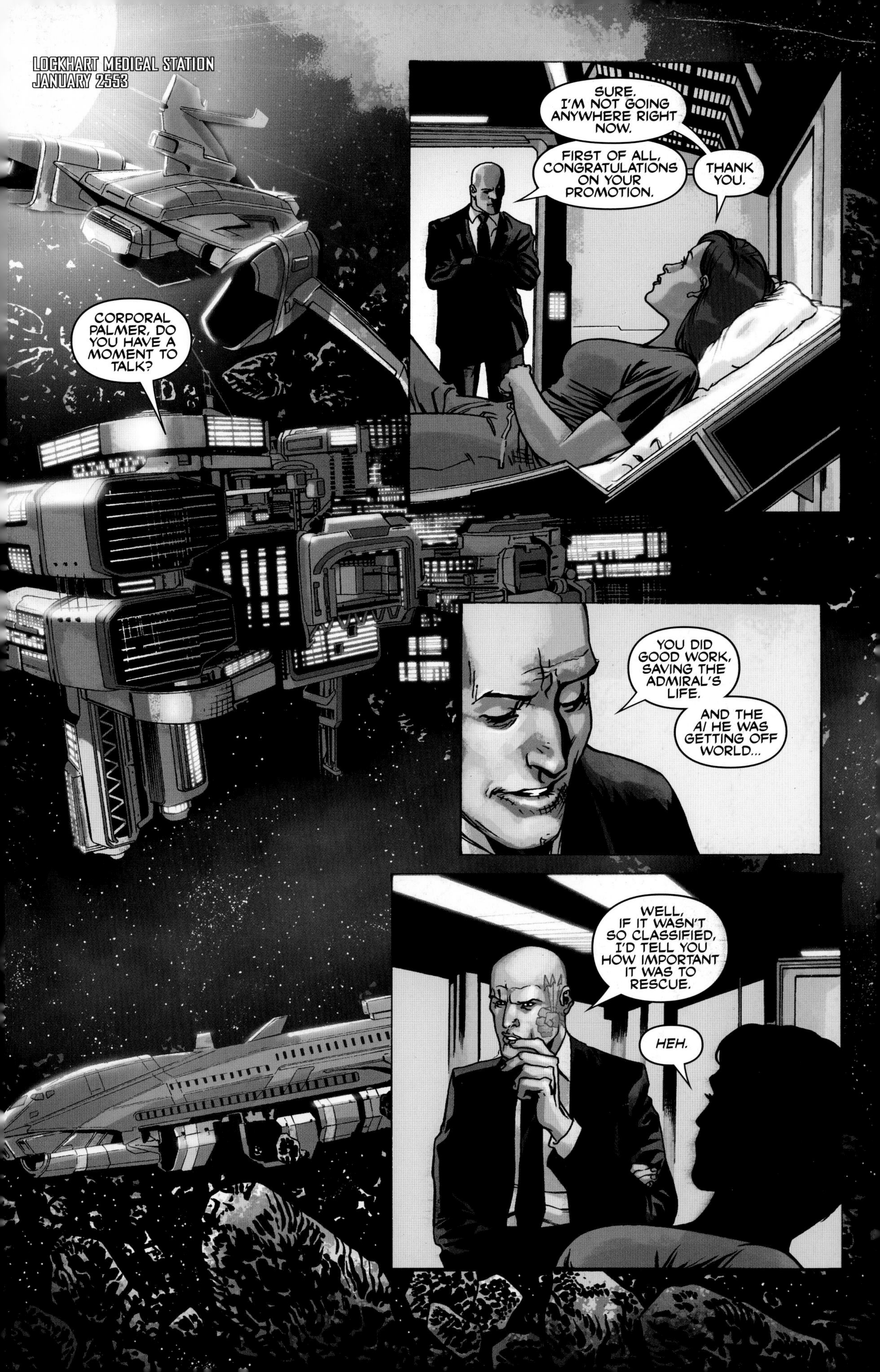
LOCKHART MEDICAL STATION
JANUARY 2553
CORPORAL PALMER, DO YOU HAVE A MOMENT TO TALK?
SURE. I'M NOT GOING ANYWHERE RIGHT NOW.
FIRST OF ALL, CONGRATULATIONS ON YOUR PROMOTION.
THANK YOU.
YOU DID GOOD WORK, SAVING THE ADMIRAL'S LIFE.
AND THE AI HE WAS GETTING OFF WORLD...
WELL, IF IT WASN'T SO CLASSIFIED, I'D TELL YOU HOW IMPORTANT IT WAS TO RESCUE.
HEH.

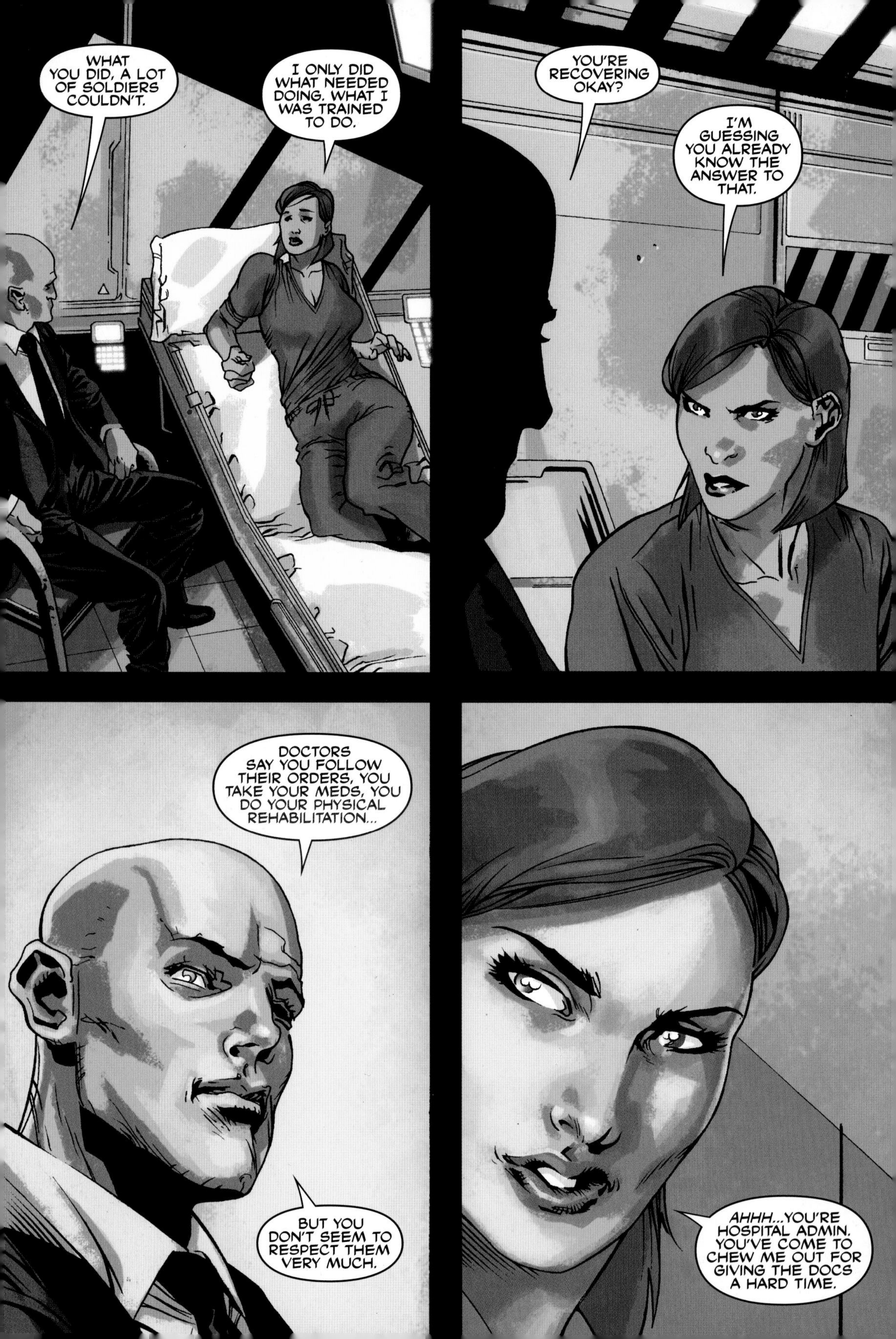

WHAT YOU DID, A LOT OF SOLDIERS COULDN'T.
I ONLY DID WHAT NEEDED DOING. WHAT I WAS TRAINED TO DO.
YOU'RE RECOVERING OKAY?
I'M GUESSING YOU ALREADY KNOW THE ANSWER TO THAT.
DOCTORS SAY YOU FOLLOW THEIR ORDERS, YOU TAKE YOUR MEDS, YOU DO YOUR PHYSICAL REHABILITATION...
BUT YOU DON'T SEEM TO RESPECT THEM VERY MUCH.
AHHH...YOU'RE HOSPITAL ADMIN. YOU'VE COME TO CHEW ME OUT FOR GIVING THE DOCS A HARD TIME.

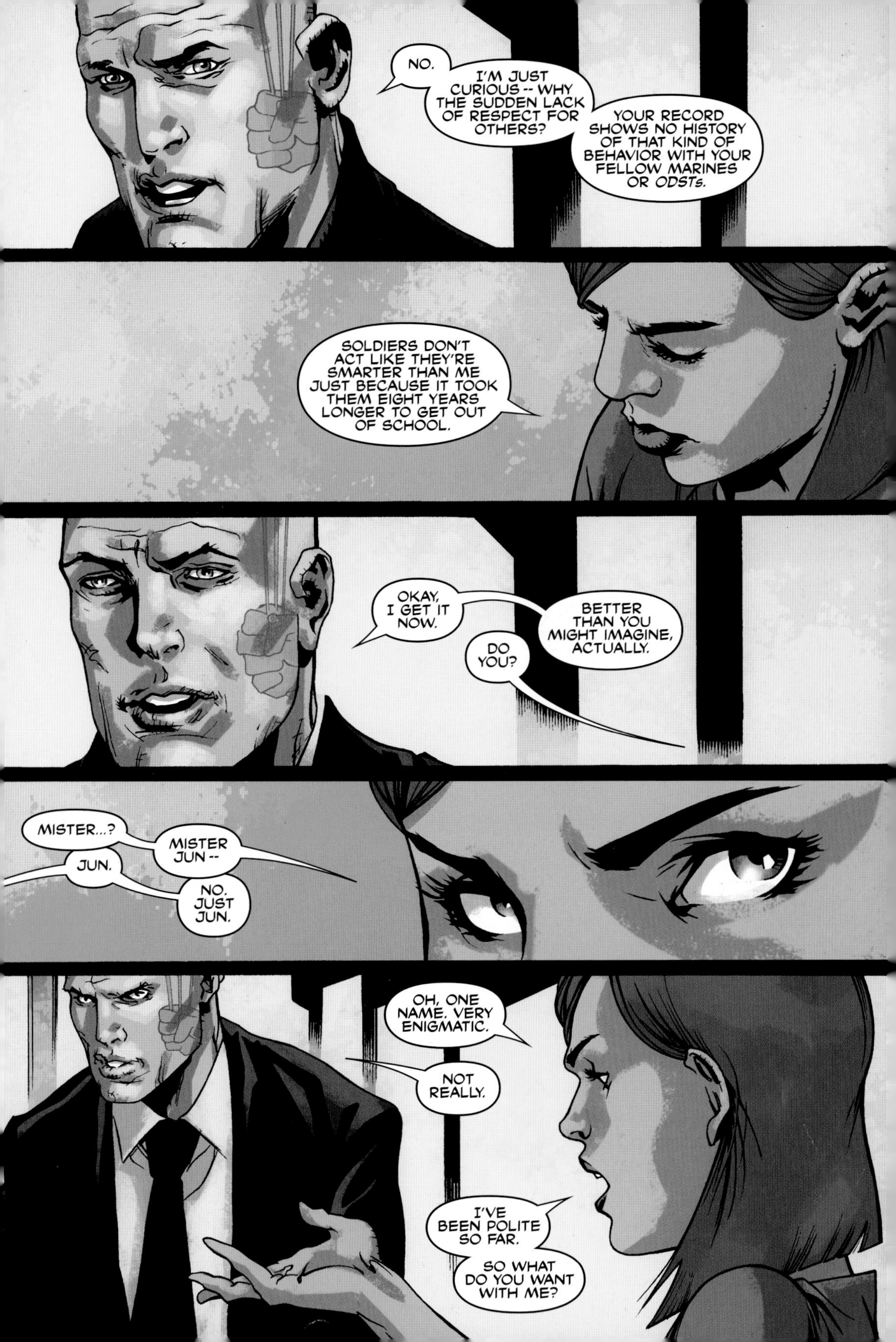
NO.
I'M JUST CURIOUS -- WHY THE SUDDEN LACK OF RESPECT FOR OTHERS?
YOUR RECORD SHOWS NO HISTORY OF THAT KIND OF BEHAVIOR WITH YOUR FELLOW MARINES OR *ODSTs*.
SOLDIERS DON'T ACT LIKE THEY'RE SMARTER THAN ME JUST BECAUSE IT TOOK THEM EIGHT YEARS LONGER TO GET OUT OF SCHOOL.
OKAY, I GET IT NOW.
DO YOU?
BETTER THAN YOU MIGHT IMAGINE, ACTUALLY.
MISTER...?
MISTER JUN --
JUN.
NO. JUST JUN.
OH, ONE NAME. VERY ENIGMATIC.
NOT REALLY.
I'VE BEEN POLITE SO FAR.
SO WHAT DO YOU WANT WITH ME?

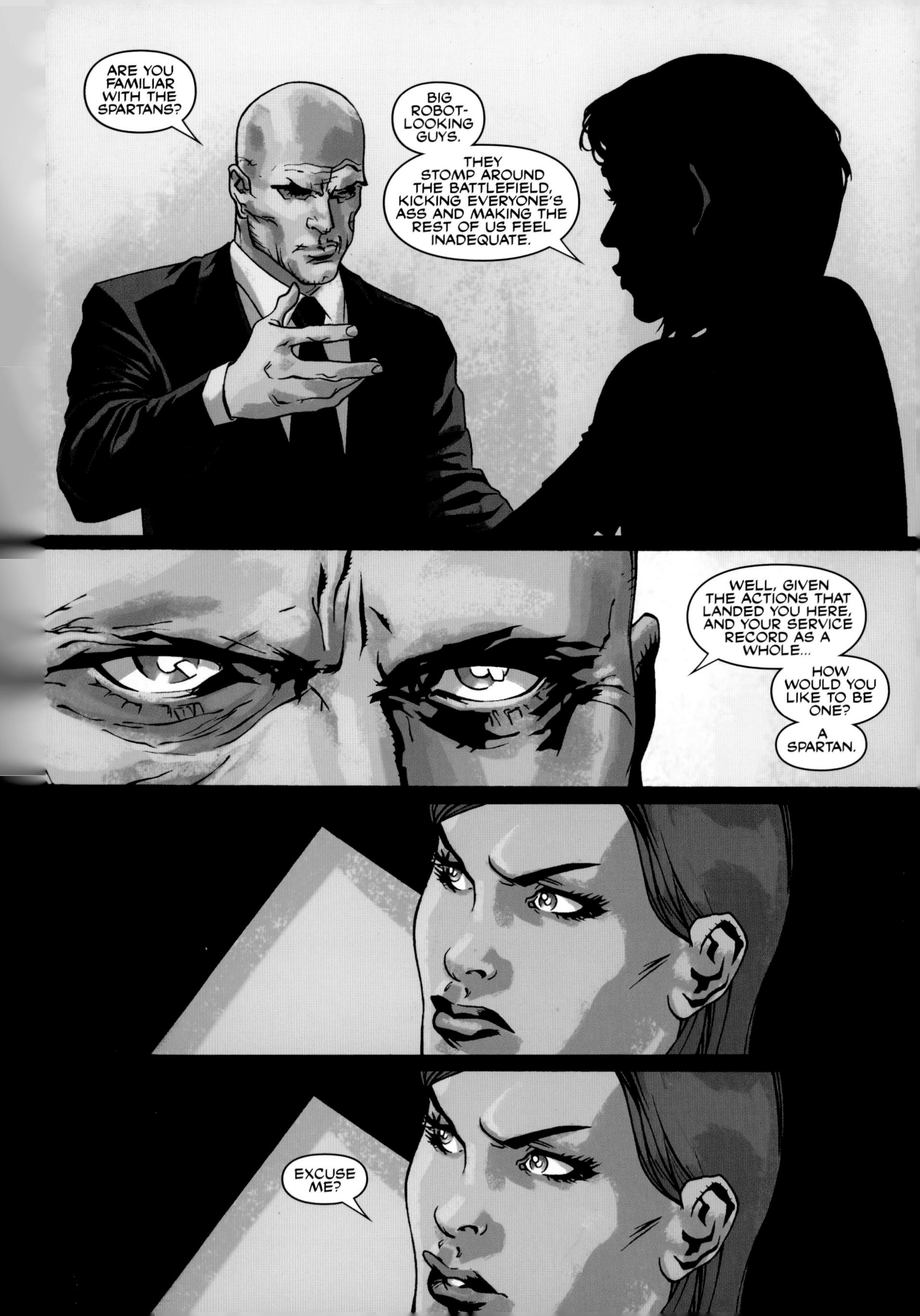
ARE YOU FAMILIAR WITH THE SPARTANS?
BIG ROBOT-LOOKING GUYS.
THEY STOMP AROUND THE BATTLEFIELD, KICKING EVERYONE'S ASS AND MAKING THE REST OF US FEEL INADEQUATE.
WELL, GIVEN THE ACTIONS THAT LANDED YOU HERE, AND YOUR SERVICE RECORD AS A WHOLE...
HOW WOULD YOU LIKE TO BE ONE?
A SPARTAN.
EXCUSE ME?

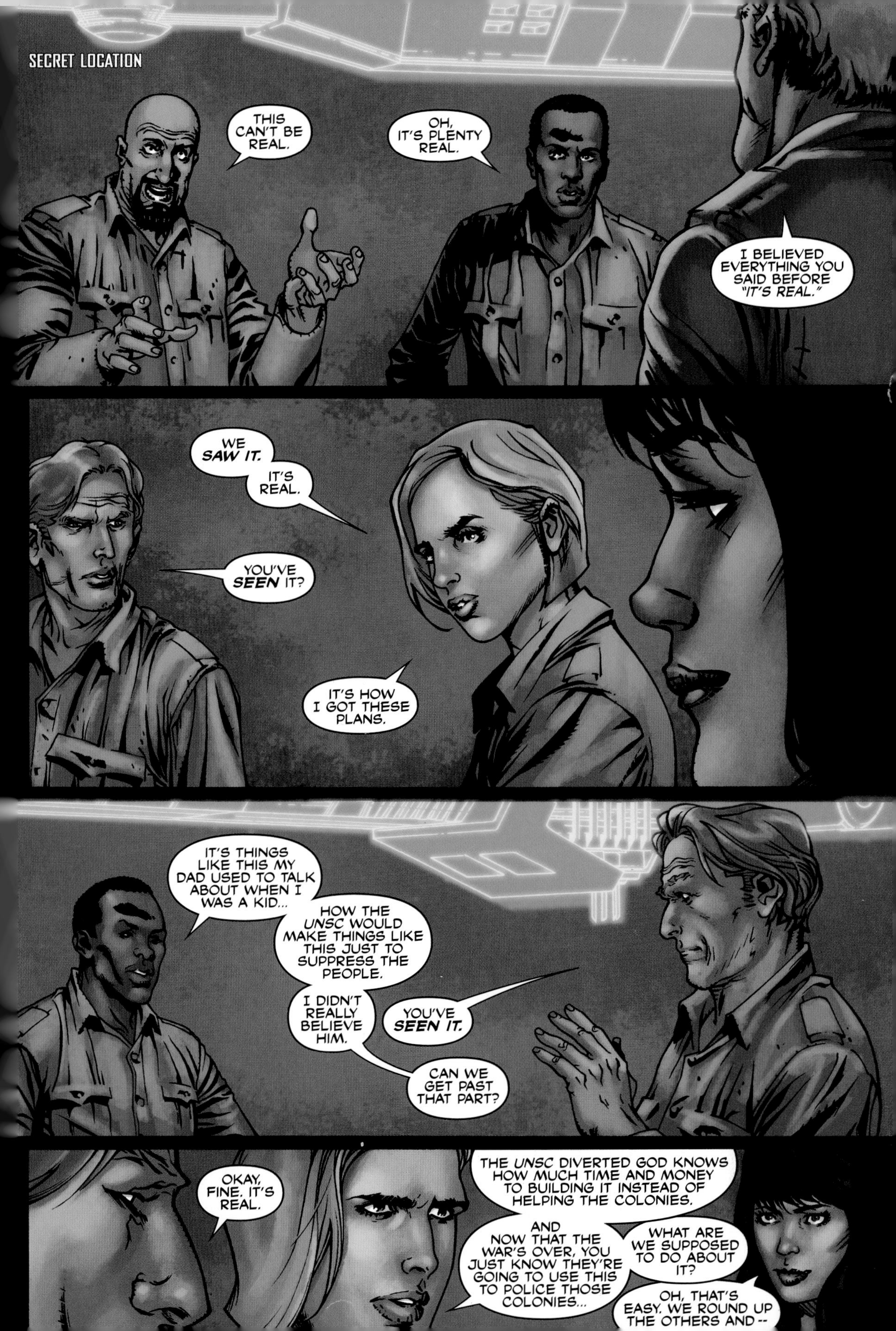
SECRET LOCATION
THIS CAN'T BE REAL.
OH, IT'S PLENTY REAL.
I BELIEVED EVERYTHING YOU SAID BEFORE "IT'S REAL."
WE SAW IT.
IT'S REAL.
YOU'VE SEEN IT?
IT'S HOW I GOT THESE PLANS.
IT'S THINGS LIKE THIS MY DAD USED TO TALK ABOUT WHEN I WAS A KID...
HOW THE UNSC WOULD MAKE THINGS LIKE THIS JUST TO SUPPRESS THE PEOPLE.
I DIDN'T REALLY BELIEVE HIM.
YOU'VE SEEN IT.
CAN WE GET PAST THAT PART?
OKAY, FINE. IT'S REAL.
THE UNSC DIVERTED GOD KNOWS HOW MUCH TIME AND MONEY TO BUILDING IT INSTEAD OF HELPING THE COLONIES.
AND NOW THAT THE WAR'S OVER, YOU JUST KNOW THEY'RE GOING TO USE THIS TO POLICE THOSE COLONIES...
WHAT ARE WE SUPPOSED TO DO ABOUT IT?
OH, THAT'S EASY. WE ROUND UP THE OTHERS AND--

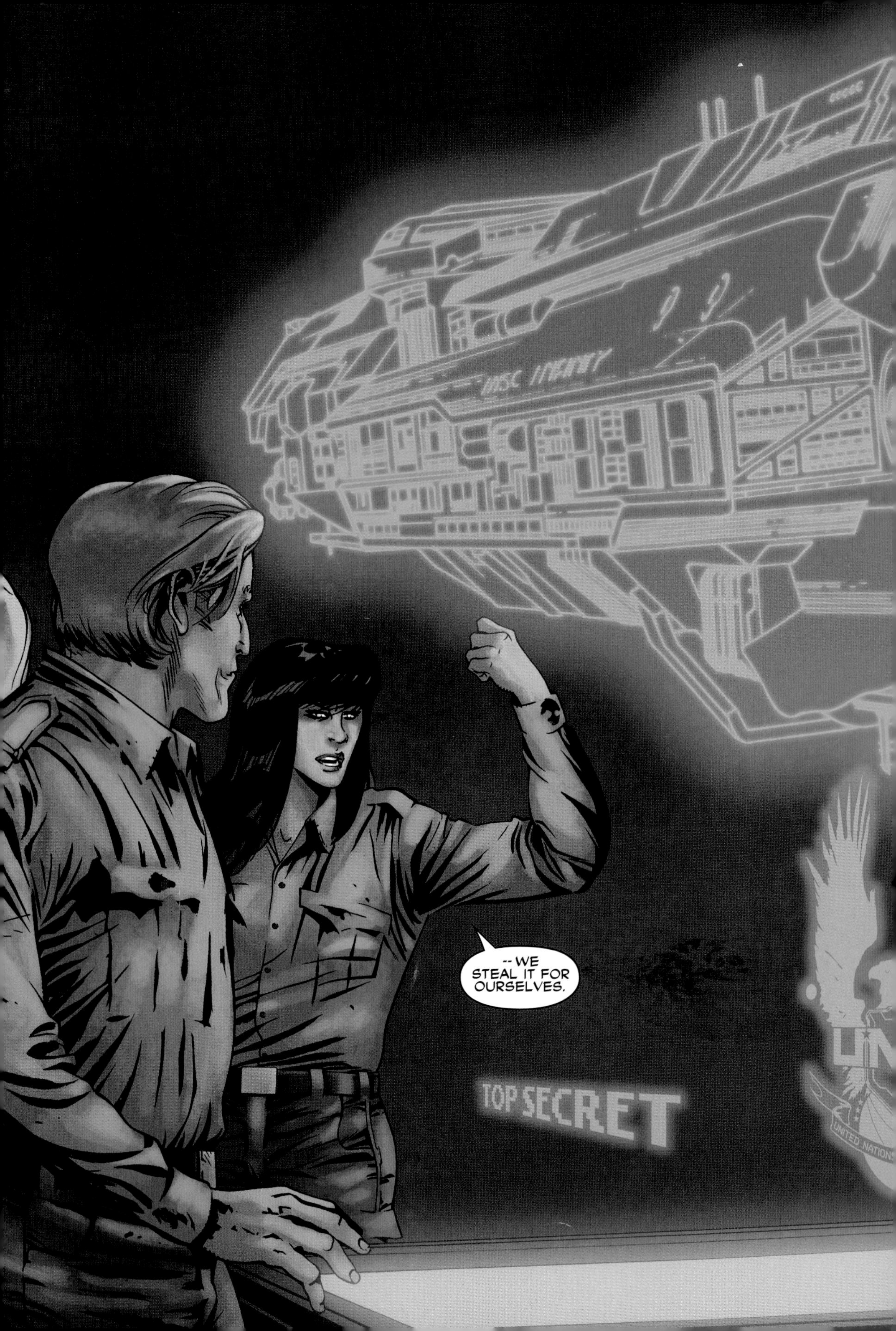
UNSC INFINITY
-- WE STEAL IT FOR OURSELVES.
TOP SECRET

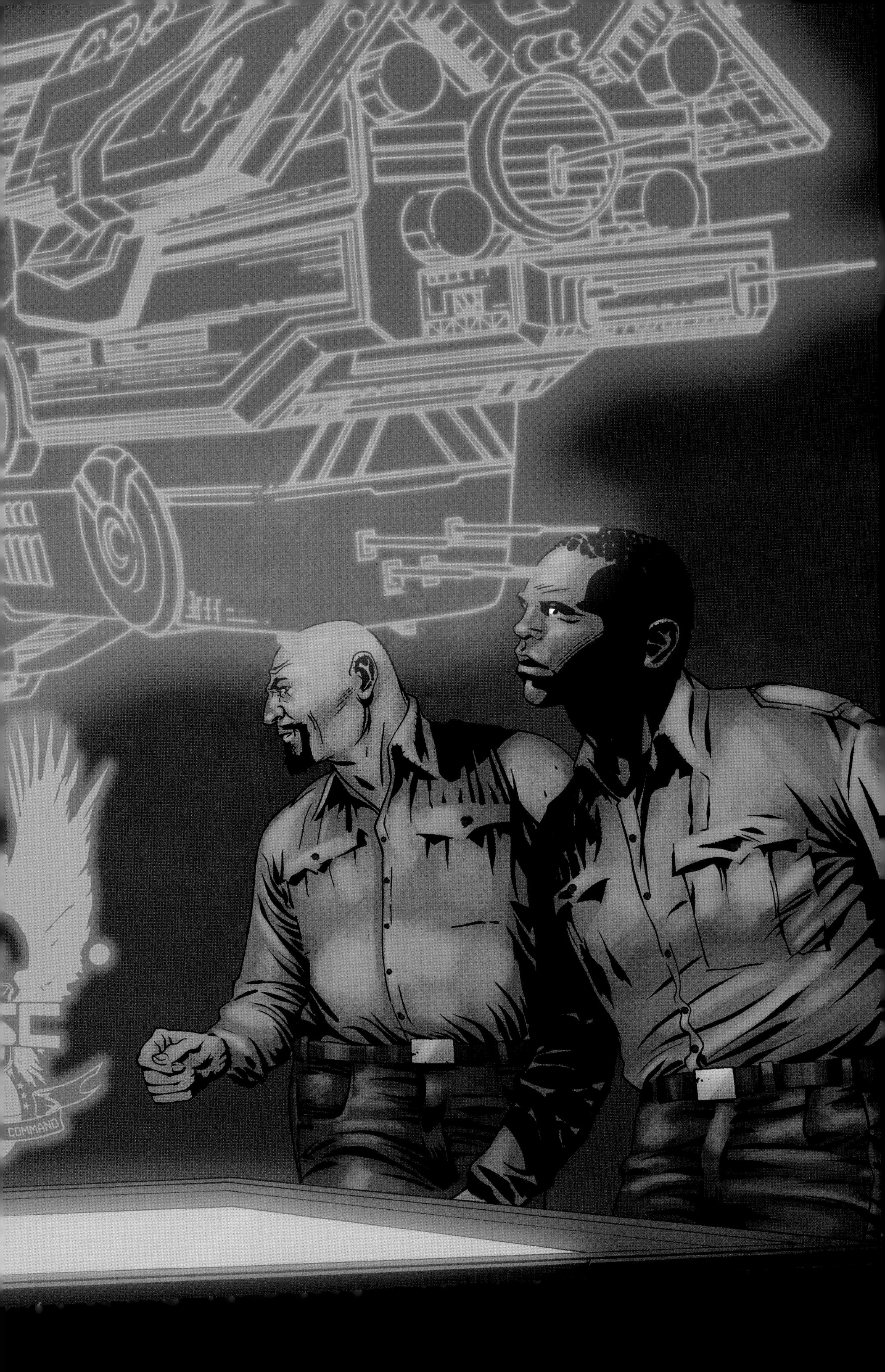
COMMAND

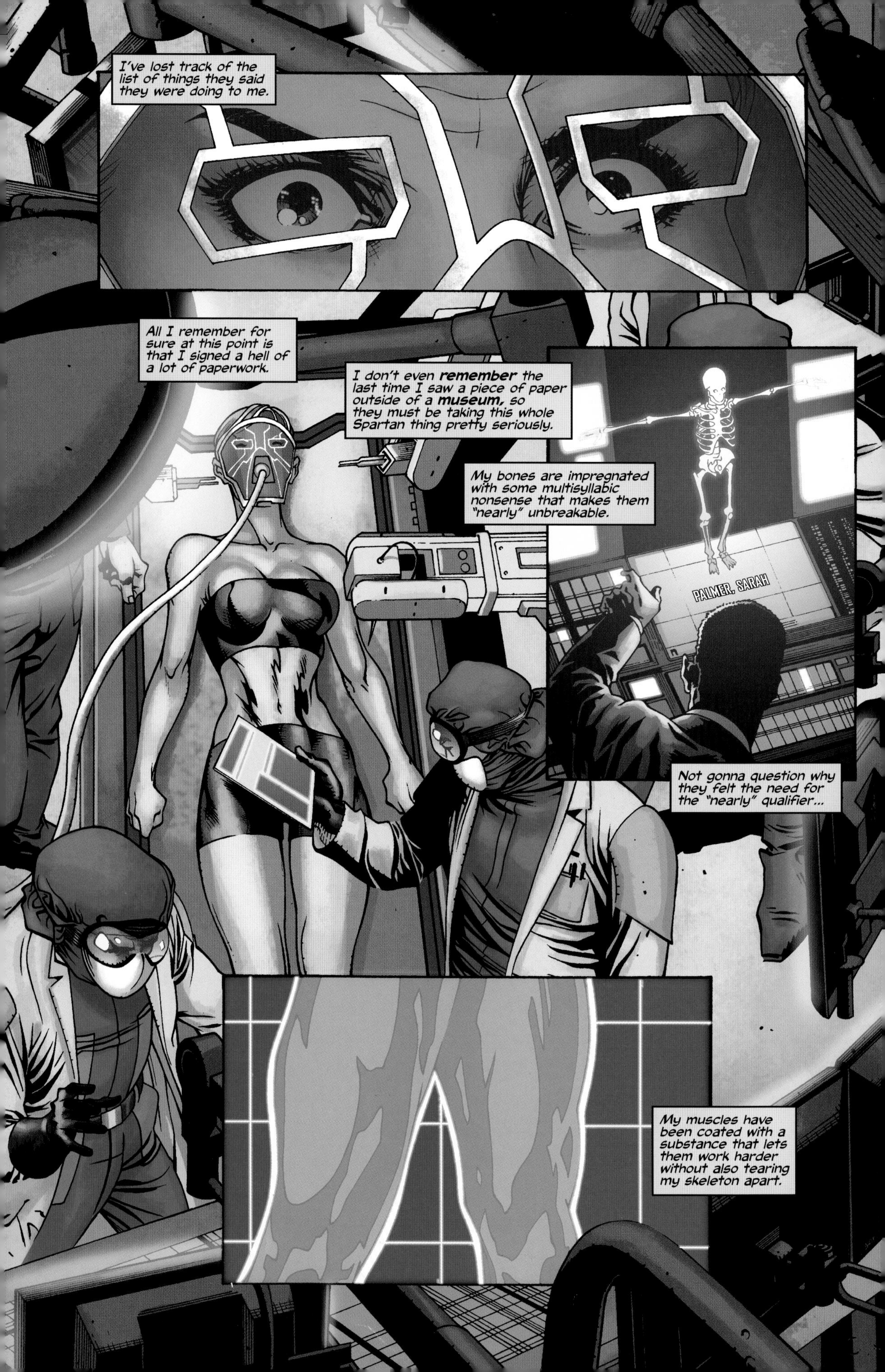
I've lost track of the list of things they said they were doing to me.
All I remember for sure at this point is that I signed a hell of a lot of paperwork.
I don't even **remember** the last time I saw a piece of paper outside of a **museum,** so they must be taking this whole Spartan thing pretty seriously.
My bones are impregnated with some multisyllabic nonsense that makes them "nearly" unbreakable.
PALMER, SARAH
Not gonna question why they felt the need for the "nearly" qualifier...
My muscles have been coated with a substance that lets them work harder without also tearing my skeleton apart.

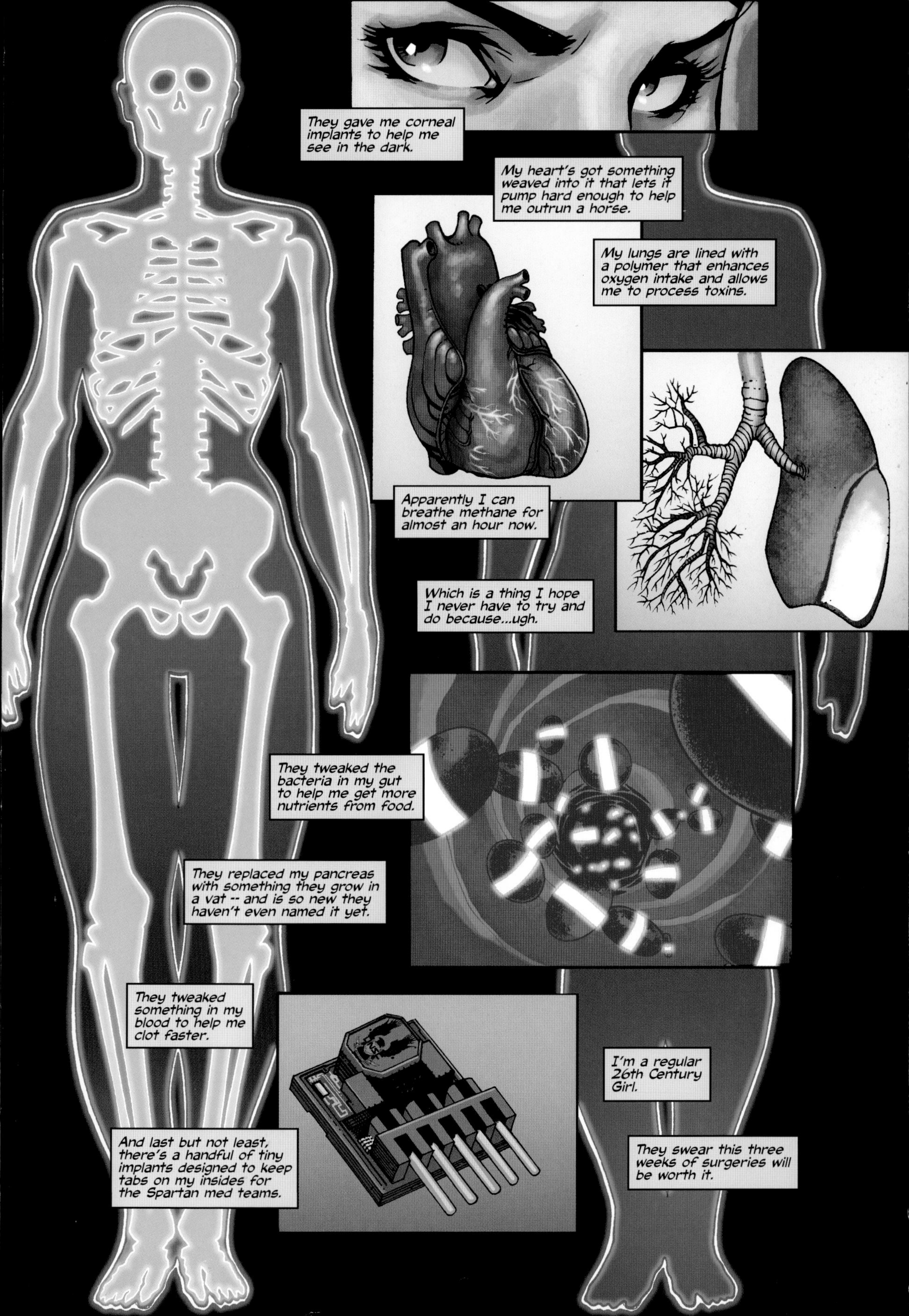
They gave me corneal implants to help me see in the dark.
My heart's got something weaved into it that lets it pump hard enough to help me outrun a horse.
My lungs are lined with a polymer that enhances oxygen intake and allows me to process toxins.
Apparently I can breathe methane for almost an hour now.
Which is a thing I hope I never have to try and do because...ugh.
They tweaked the bacteria in my gut to help me get more nutrients from food.
They replaced my pancreas with something they grow in a vat -- and is so new they haven't even named it yet.
They tweaked something in my blood to help me clot faster.
I'm a regular 26th Century Girl.
And last but not least, there's a handful of tiny implants designed to keep tabs on my insides for the Spartan med teams.
They swear this three weeks of surgeries will be worth it.

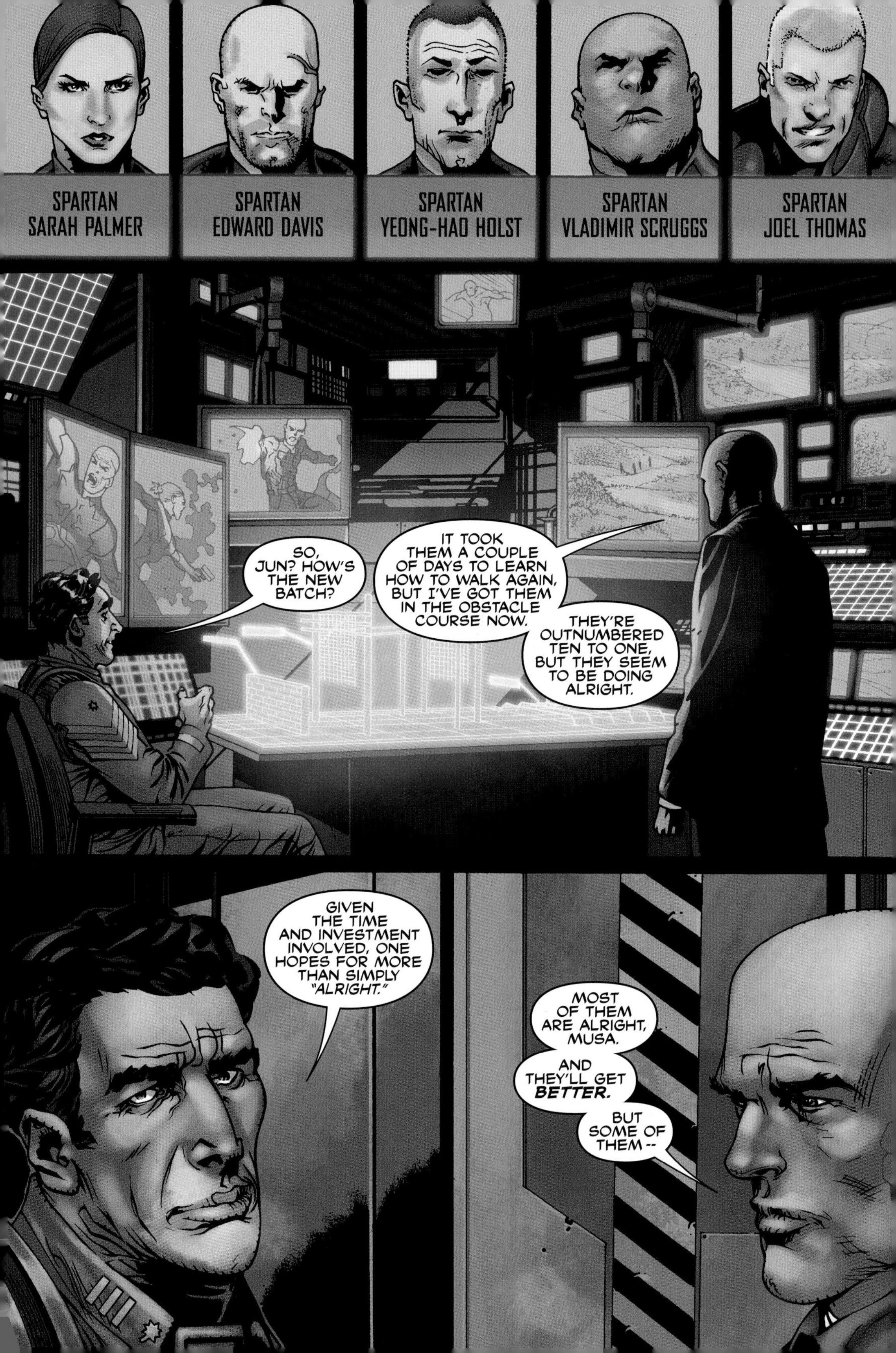
SPARTAN SARAH PALMER
SPARTAN EDWARD DAVIS
SPARTAN YEONG-HAO HOLST
SPARTAN VLADIMIR SCRUGGS
SPARTAN JOEL THOMAS
SO, JUN? HOW'S THE NEW BATCH?
IT TOOK THEM A COUPLE OF DAYS TO LEARN HOW TO WALK AGAIN, BUT I'VE GOT THEM IN THE OBSTACLE COURSE NOW.
THEY'RE OUTNUMBERED TEN TO ONE, BUT THEY SEEM TO BE DOING ALRIGHT.
GIVEN THE TIME AND INVESTMENT INVOLVED, ONE HOPES FOR MORE THAN SIMPLY *"ALRIGHT."*
MOST OF THEM ARE ALRIGHT, MUSA.
AND THEY'LL GET ***BETTER.***
BUT SOME OF THEM --

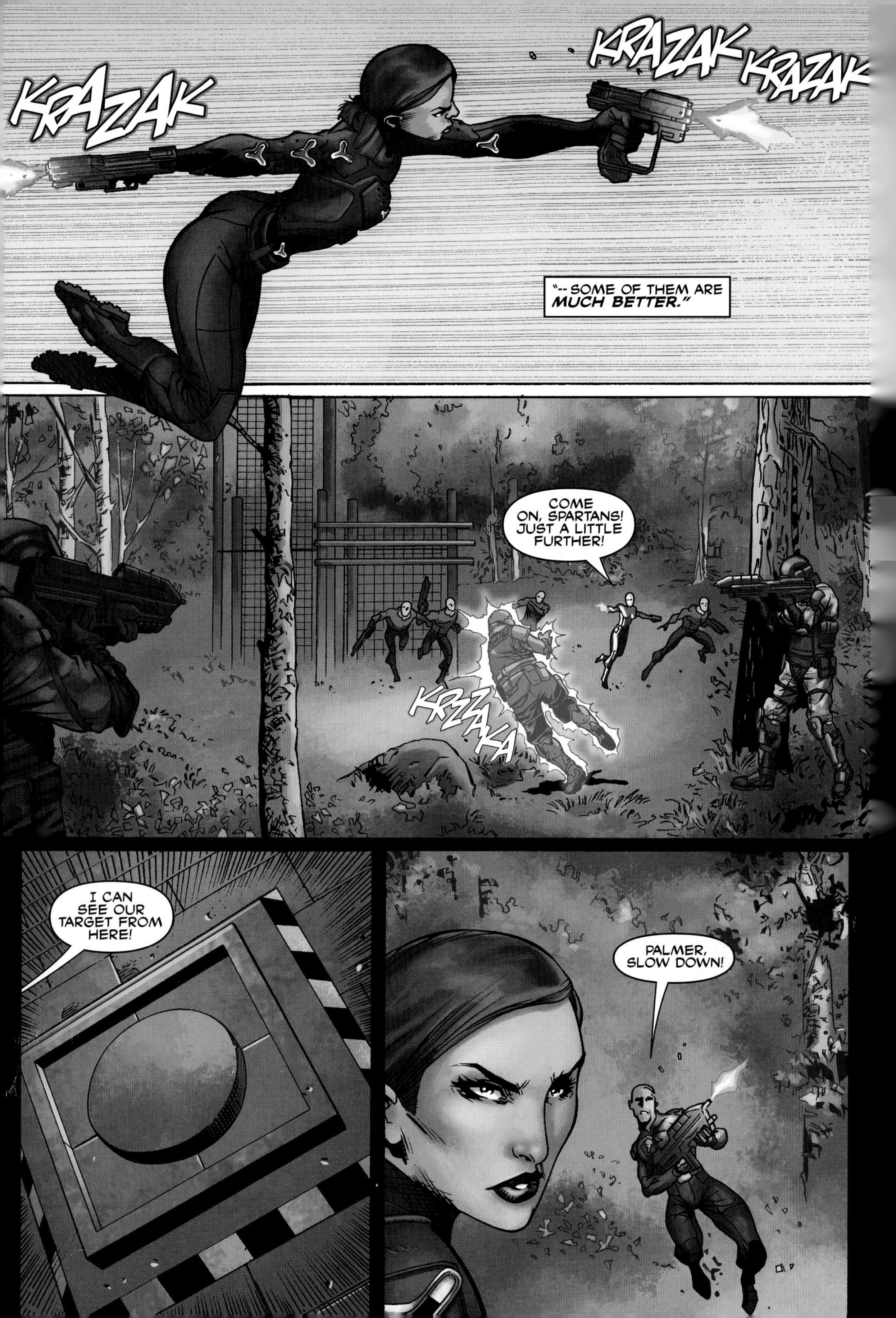
KRAZAK
KRAZAK KRAZAK
"-- SOME OF THEM ARE MUCH BETTER."
COME ON, SPARTANS! JUST A LITTLE FURTHER!
KRZZAKA
I CAN SEE OUR TARGET FROM HERE!
PALMER, SLOW DOWN!

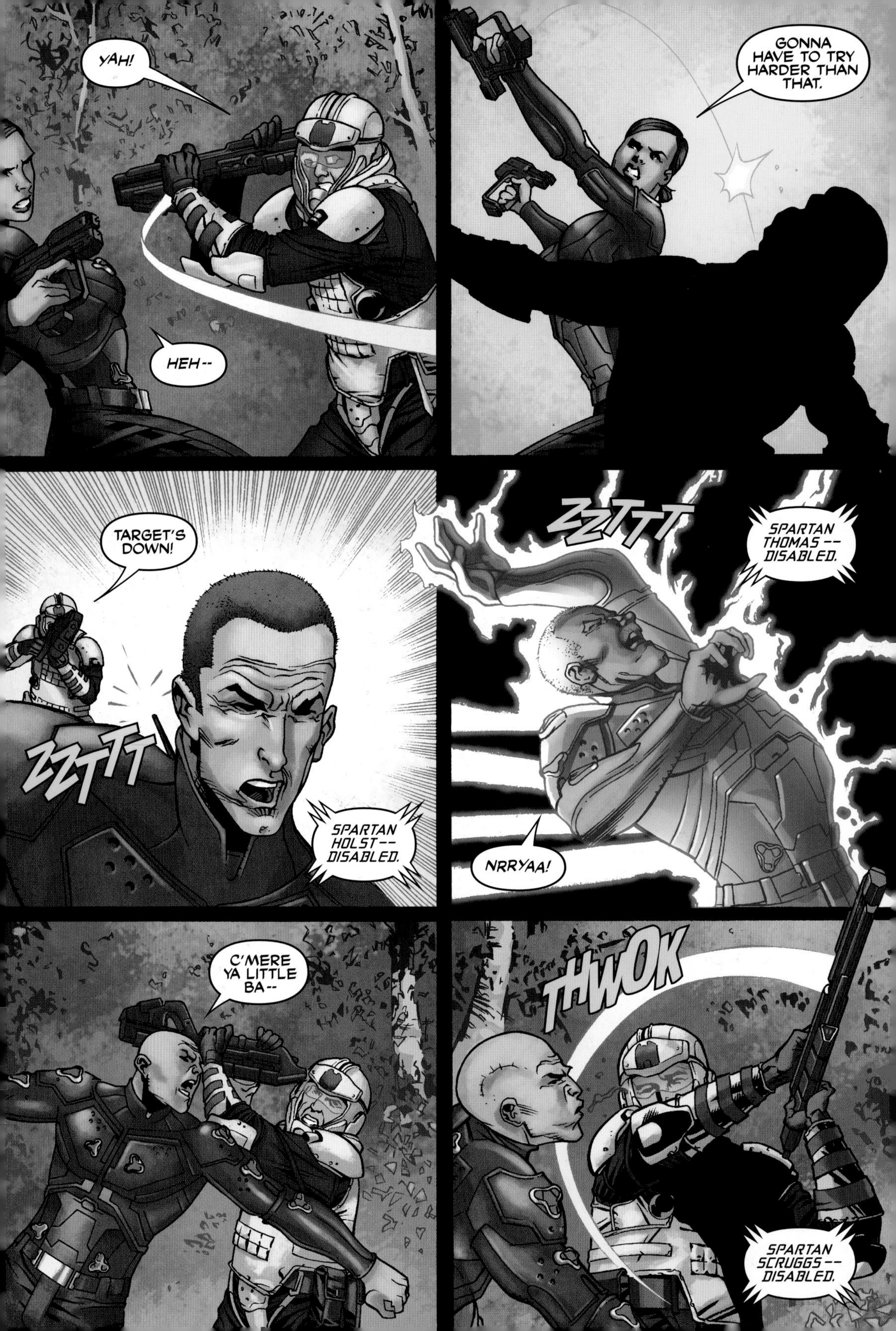
YAH!
HEH--
GONNA HAVE TO TRY HARDER THAN THAT.
TARGET'S DOWN!
ZZTTTT
SPARTAN HOLST-- DISABLED.
ZZTTTT
SPARTAN THOMAS-- DISABLED.
NRRYAA!
C'MERE YA LITTLE BA--
THWOK
SPARTAN SCRUGGS-- DISABLED.

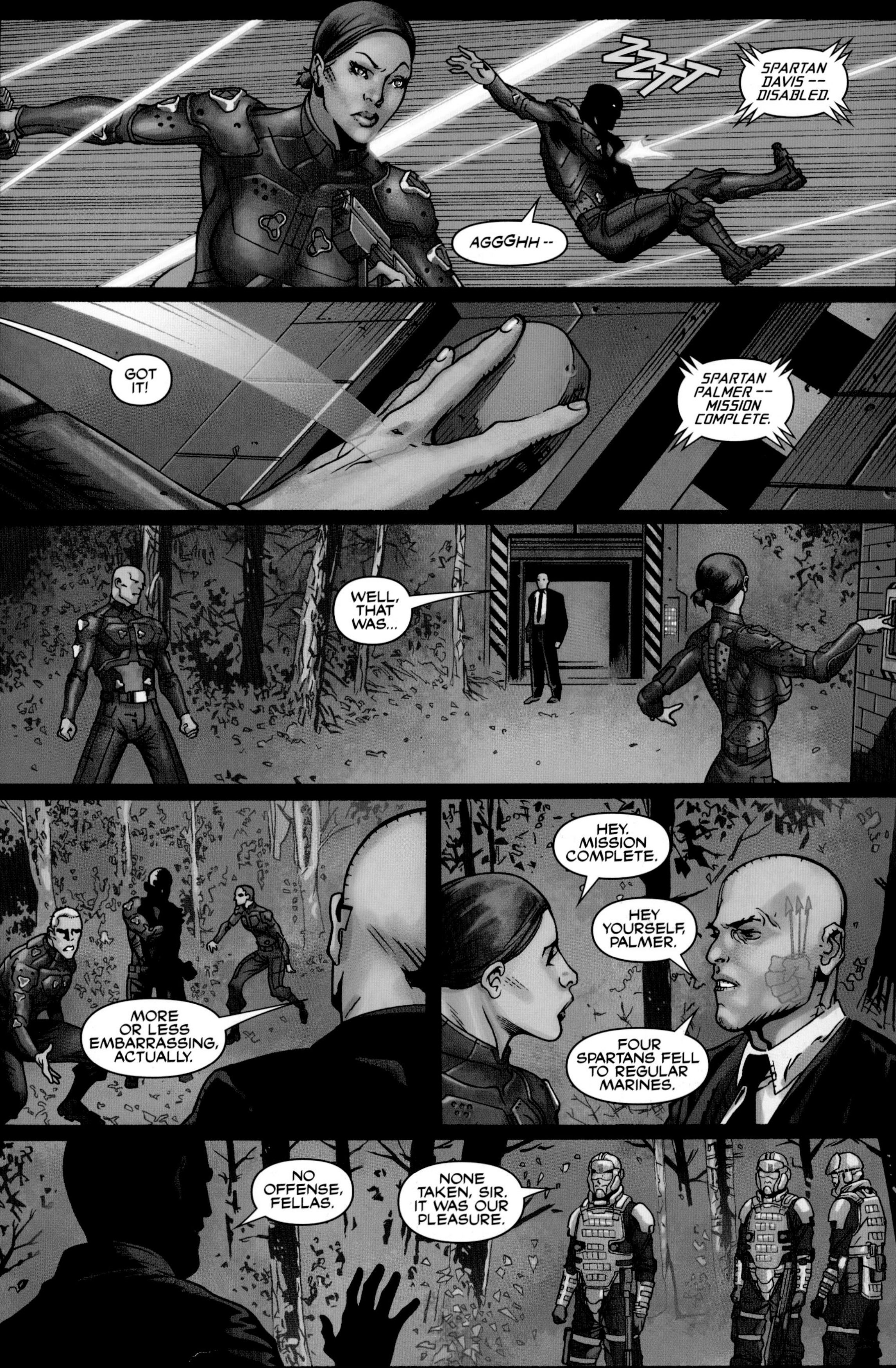
ZZZT
SPARTAN DAVIS -- DISABLED.
AGGGHH --
GOT IT!
SPARTAN PALMER -- MISSION COMPLETE.
WELL, THAT WAS...
MORE OR LESS EMBARRASSING, ACTUALLY.
HEY. MISSION COMPLETE.
HEY YOURSELF, PALMER.
FOUR SPARTANS FELL TO REGULAR MARINES.
NO OFFENSE, FELLAS.
NONE TAKEN, SIR. IT WAS OUR PLEASURE.

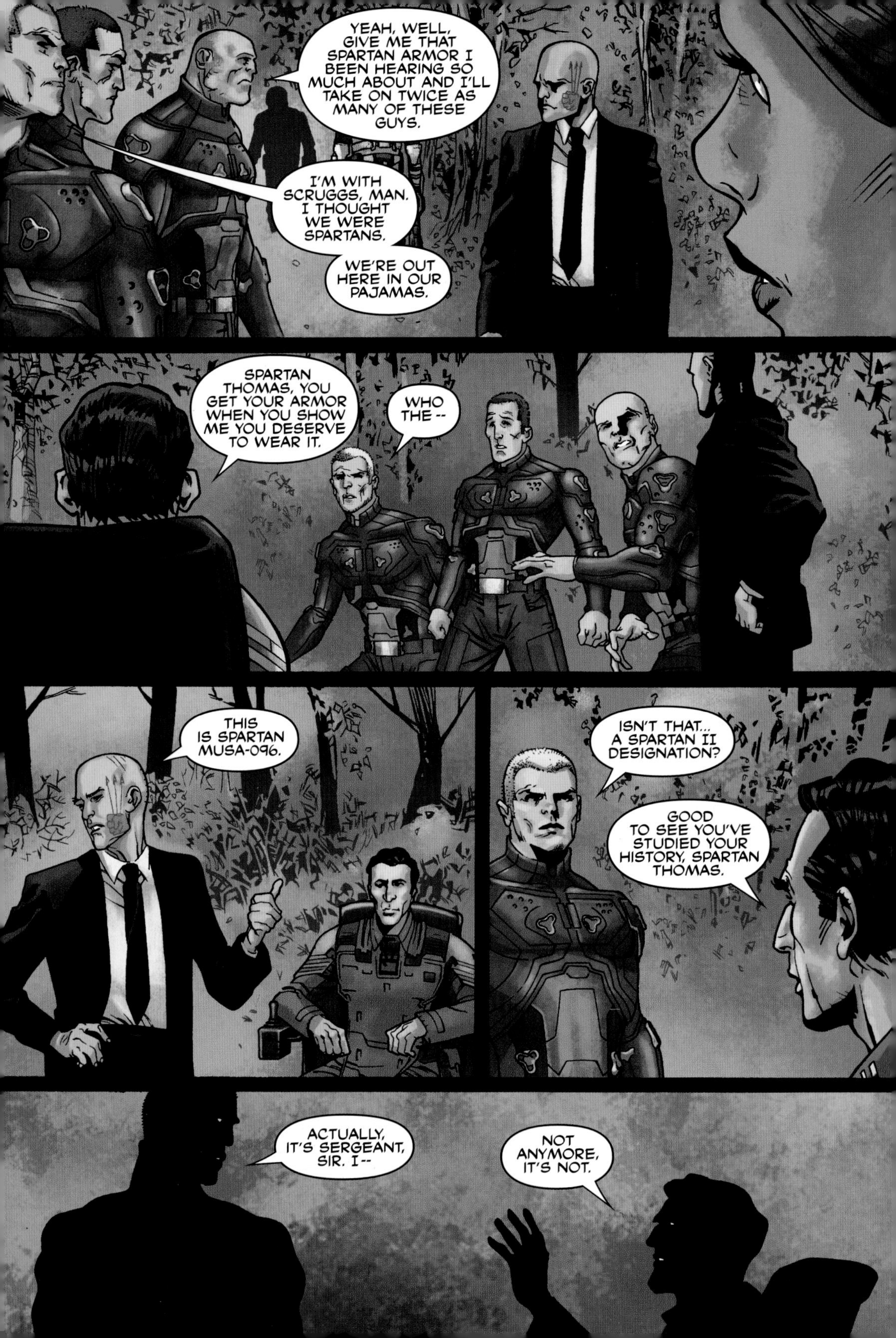
YEAH, WELL, GIVE ME THAT SPARTAN ARMOR I BEEN HEARING SO MUCH ABOUT AND I'LL TAKE ON TWICE AS MANY OF THESE GUYS.
I'M WITH SCRUGGS, MAN. I THOUGHT WE WERE SPARTANS.
WE'RE OUT HERE IN OUR PAJAMAS.
SPARTAN THOMAS, YOU GET YOUR ARMOR WHEN YOU SHOW ME YOU DESERVE TO WEAR IT.
WHO THE --
THIS IS SPARTAN MUSA-096.
ISN'T THAT... A SPARTAN II DESIGNATION?
GOOD TO SEE YOU'VE STUDIED YOUR HISTORY, SPARTAN THOMAS.
ACTUALLY, IT'S SERGEANT, SIR. I--
NOT ANYMORE, IT'S NOT.

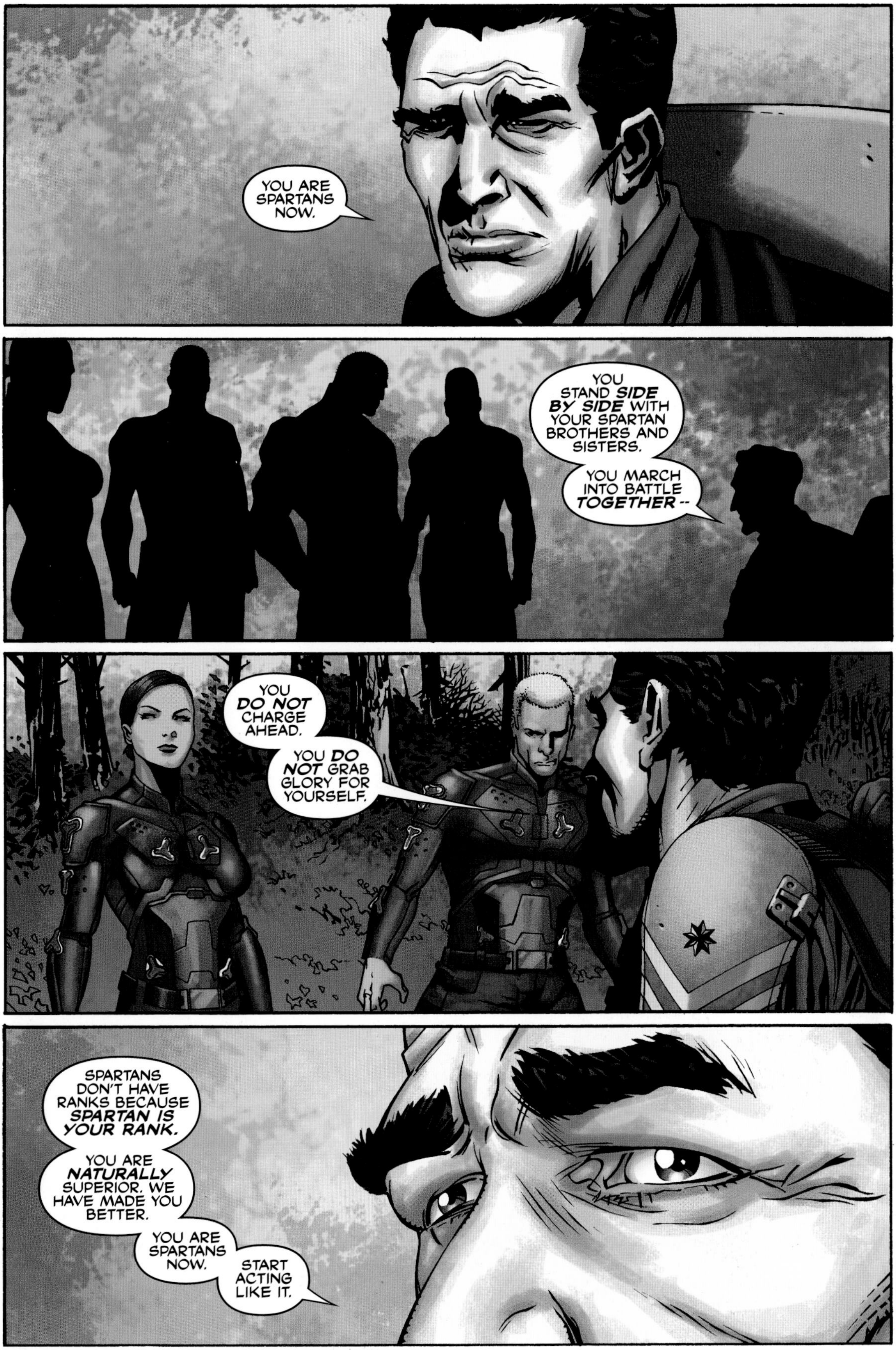
YOU ARE SPARTANS NOW.
YOU STAND SIDE BY SIDE WITH YOUR SPARTAN BROTHERS AND SISTERS.
YOU MARCH INTO BATTLE TOGETHER --
YOU DO NOT CHARGE AHEAD.
YOU DO NOT GRAB GLORY FOR YOURSELF.
SPARTANS DON'T HAVE RANKS BECAUSE SPARTAN IS YOUR RANK.
YOU ARE NATURALLY SUPERIOR. WE HAVE MADE YOU BETTER.
YOU ARE SPARTANS NOW.
START ACTING LIKE IT.

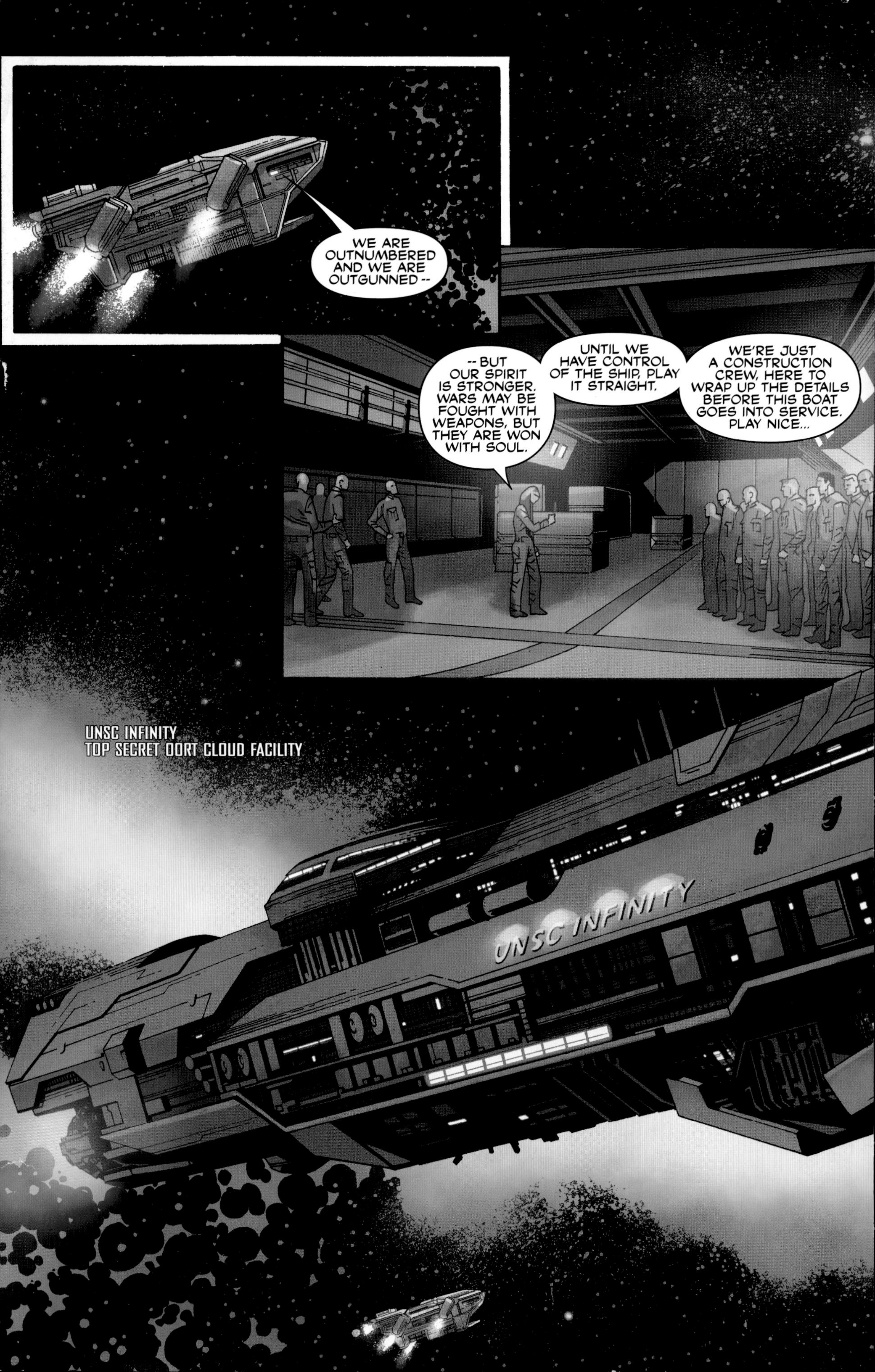
WE ARE OUTNUMBERED AND WE ARE OUTGUNNED --
-- BUT OUR SPIRIT IS STRONGER. WARS MAY BE FOUGHT WITH WEAPONS, BUT THEY ARE WON WITH SOUL.
UNTIL WE HAVE CONTROL OF THE SHIP, PLAY IT STRAIGHT.
WE'RE JUST A CONSTRUCTION CREW, HERE TO WRAP UP THE DETAILS BEFORE THIS BOAT GOES INTO SERVICE. PLAY NICE...
UNSC INFINITY
TOP SECRET OORT CLOUD FACILITY
UNSC INFINITY

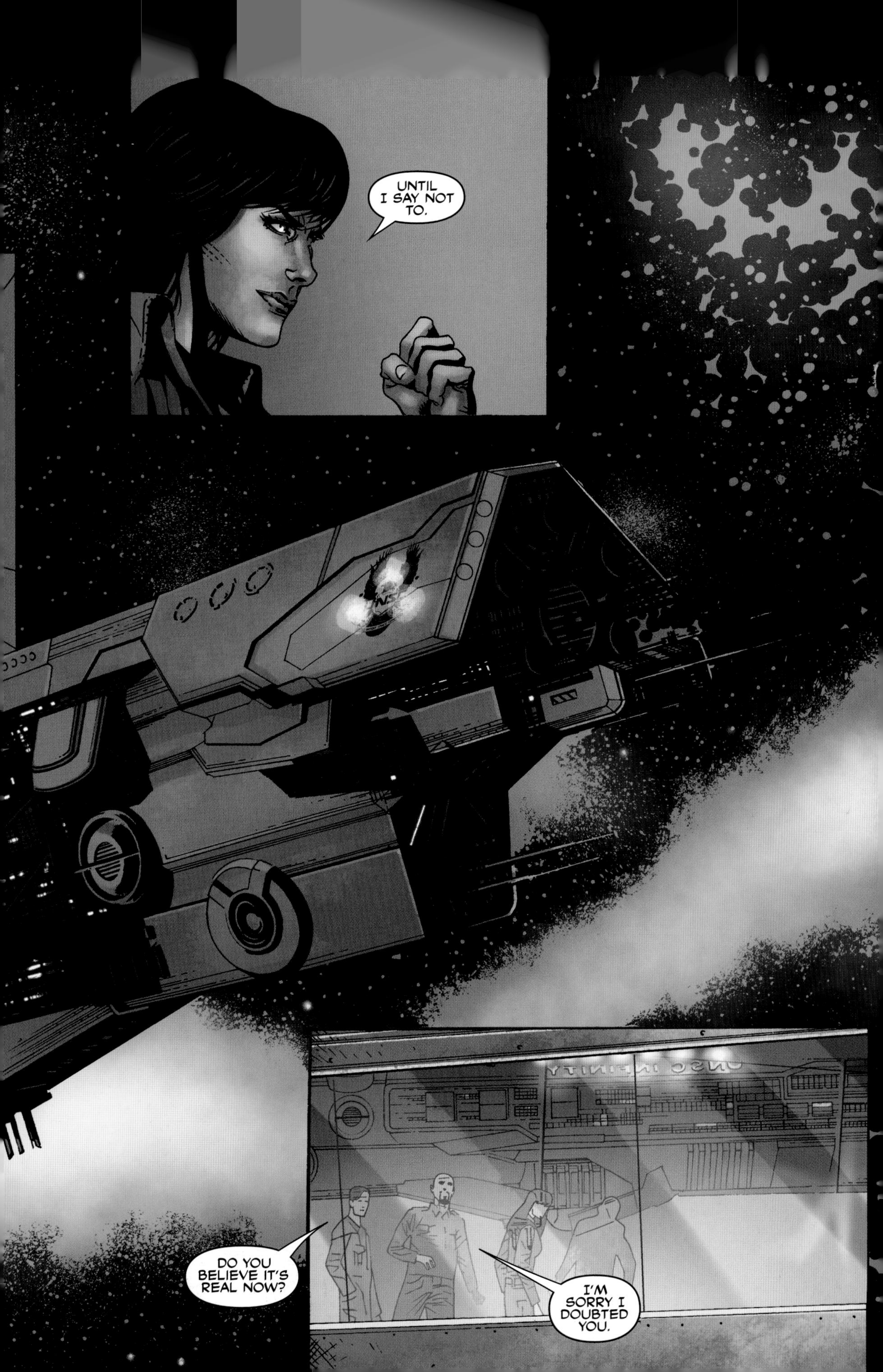
UNTIL I SAY NOT TO.
DO YOU BELIEVE IT'S REAL NOW?
I'M SORRY I DOUBTED YOU.

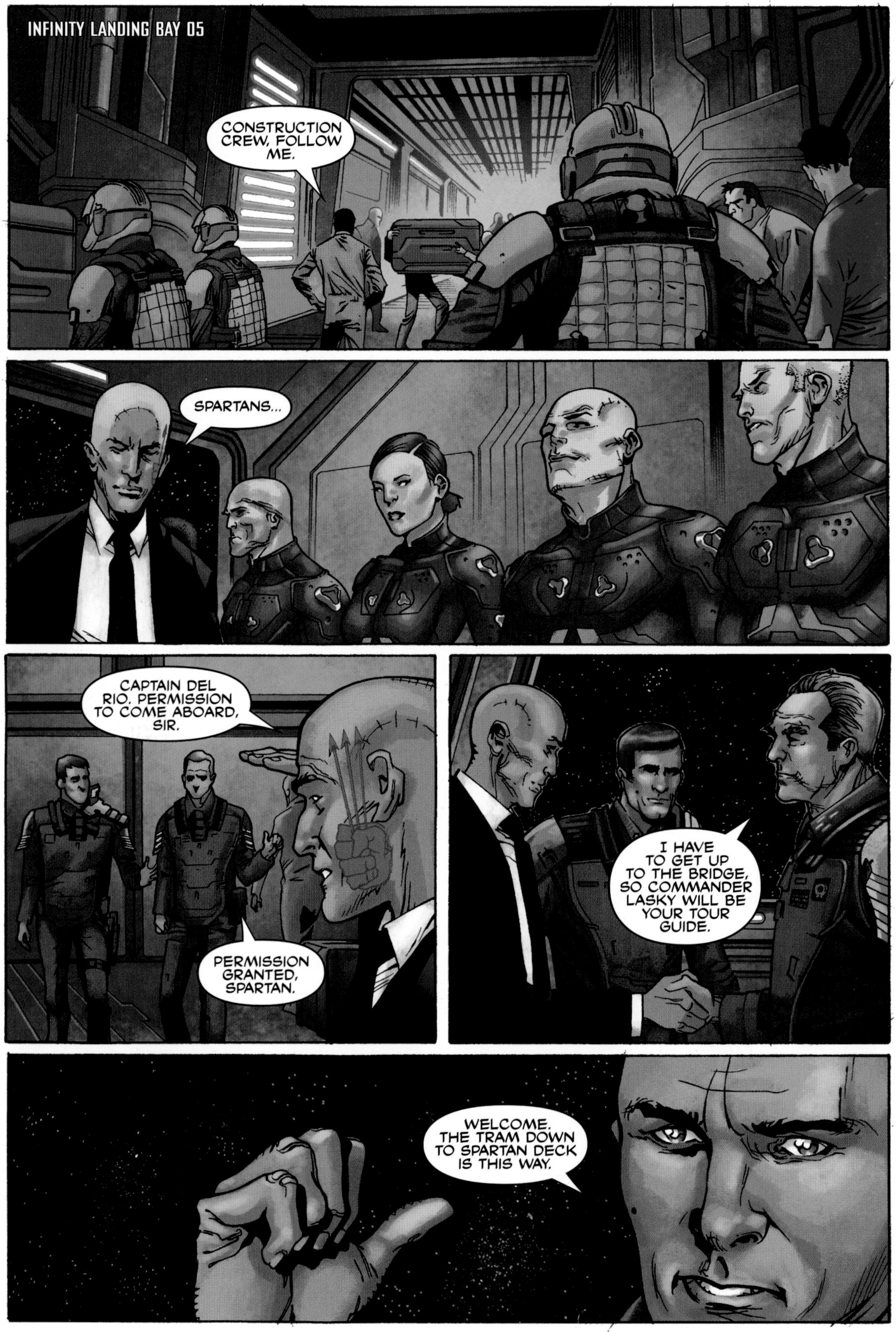
INFINITY LANDING BAY 05
CONSTRUCTION CREW, FOLLOW ME.
SPARTANS...
CAPTAIN DEL RIO. PERMISSION TO COME ABOARD, SIR.
PERMISSION GRANTED, SPARTAN.
I HAVE TO GET UP TO THE BRIDGE, SO COMMANDER LASKY WILL BE YOUR TOUR GUIDE.
WELCOME. THE TRAM DOWN TO SPARTAN DECK IS THIS WAY.

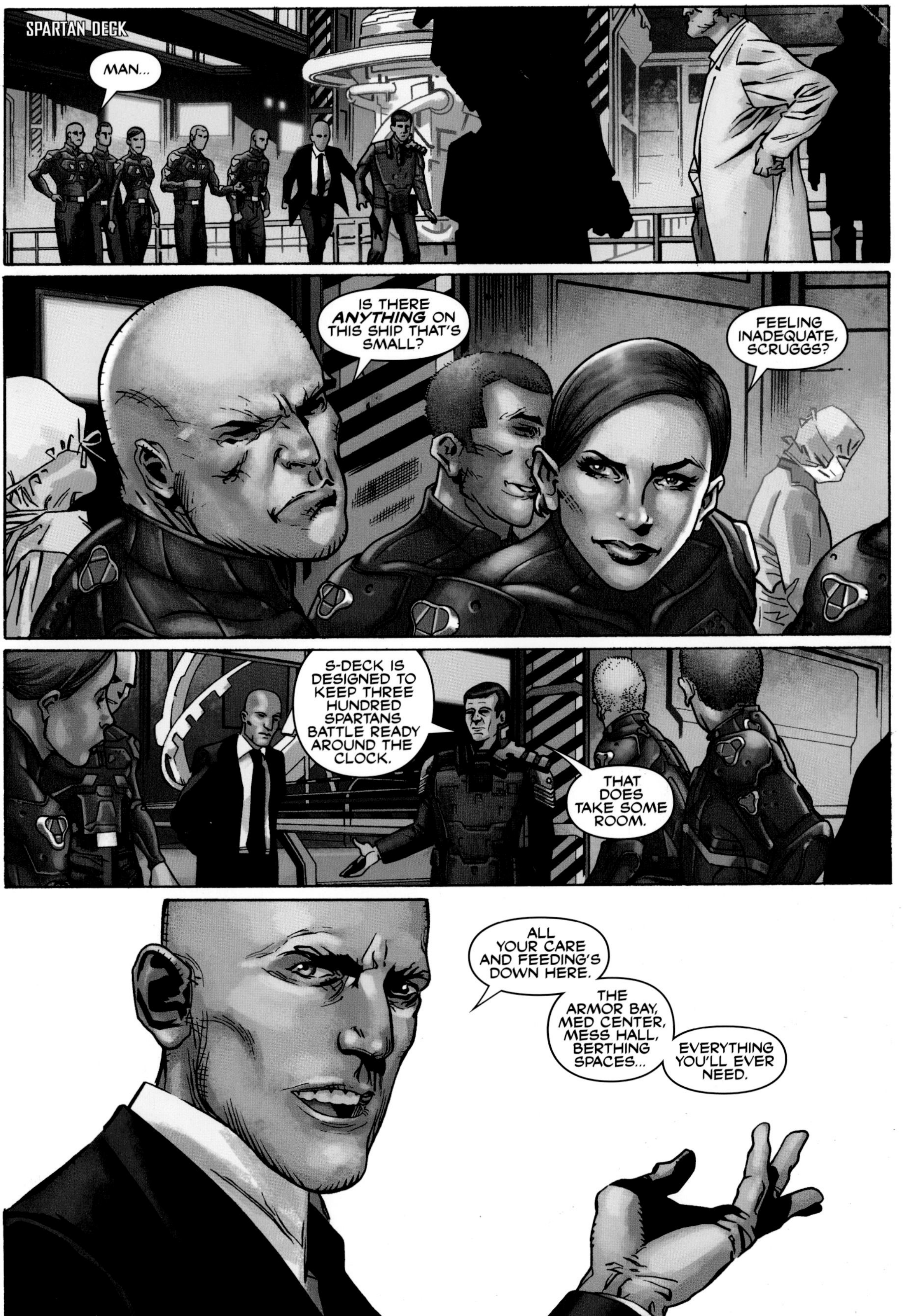
SPARTAN DECK
MAN...
IS THERE ANYTHING ON THIS SHIP THAT'S SMALL?
FEELING INADEQUATE, SCRUGGS?
S-DECK IS DESIGNED TO KEEP THREE HUNDRED SPARTANS BATTLE READY AROUND THE CLOCK.
THAT DOES TAKE SOME ROOM.
ALL YOUR CARE AND FEEDING'S DOWN HERE.
THE ARMOR BAY, MED CENTER, MESS HALL, BERTHING SPACES...
EVERYTHING YOU'LL EVER NEED.

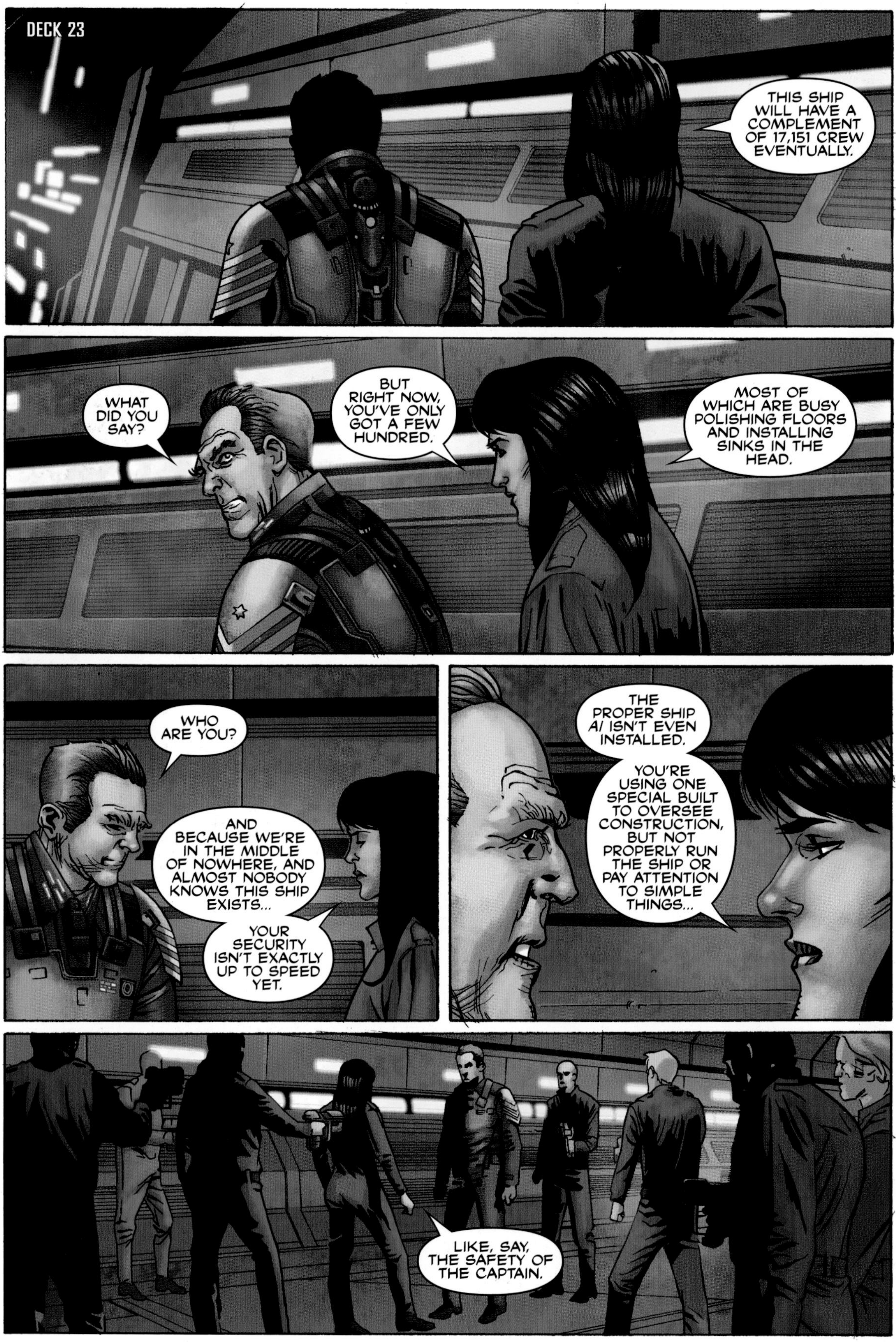
DECK 23
THIS SHIP WILL HAVE A COMPLEMENT OF 17,151 CREW EVENTUALLY.
WHAT DID YOU SAY?
BUT RIGHT NOW, YOU'VE ONLY GOT A FEW HUNDRED.
MOST OF WHICH ARE BUSY POLISHING FLOORS AND INSTALLING SINKS IN THE HEAD.
WHO ARE YOU?
AND BECAUSE WE'RE IN THE MIDDLE OF NOWHERE, AND ALMOST NOBODY KNOWS THIS SHIP EXISTS...
YOUR SECURITY ISN'T EXACTLY UP TO SPEED YET.
THE PROPER SHIP AI ISN'T EVEN INSTALLED.
YOU'RE USING ONE SPECIAL BUILT TO OVERSEE CONSTRUCTION, BUT NOT PROPERLY RUN THE SHIP OR PAY ATTENTION TO SIMPLE THINGS...
LIKE, SAY, THE SAFETY OF THE CAPTAIN.

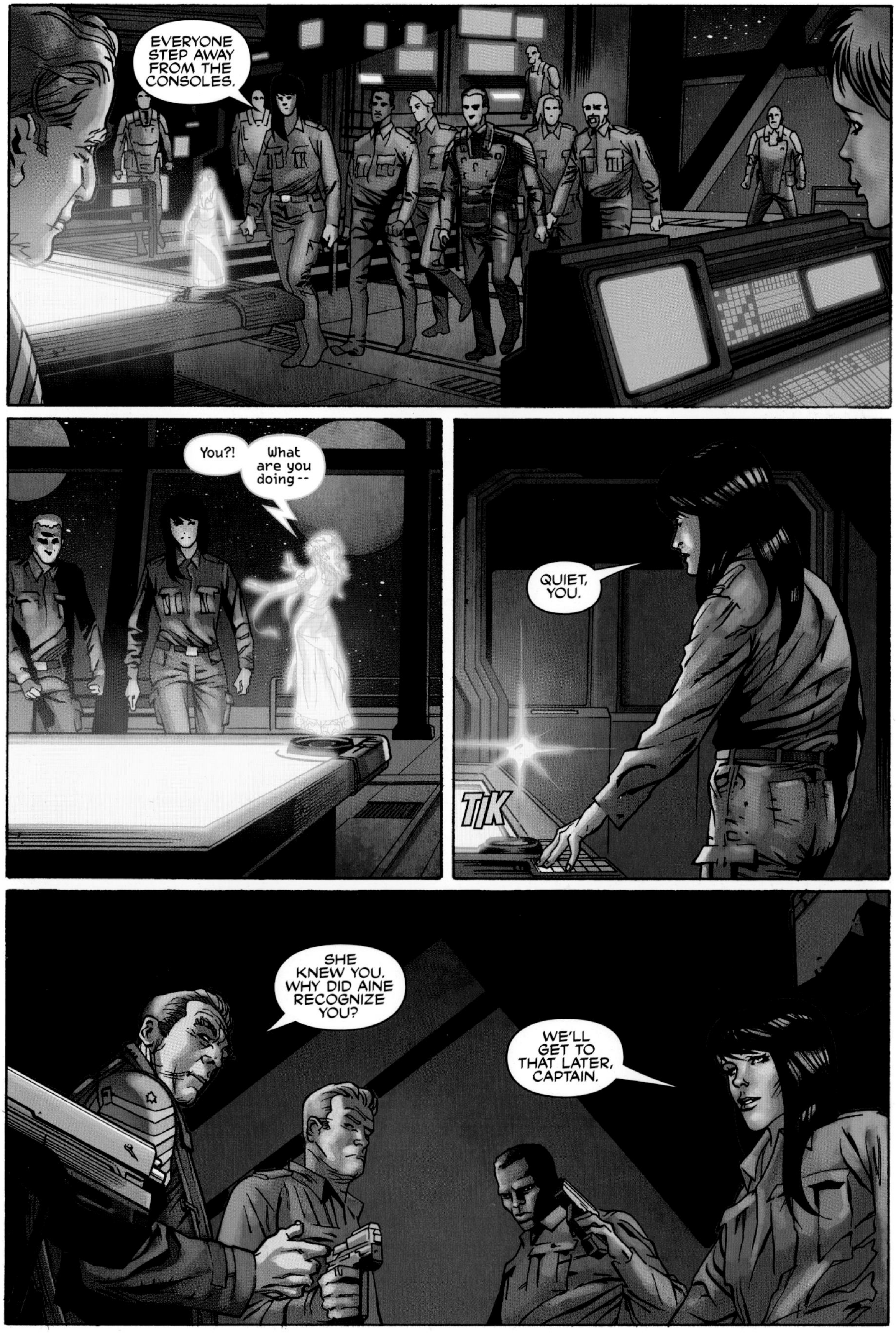
EVERYONE STEP AWAY FROM THE CONSOLES.
You?!
What are you doing --
QUIET, YOU.
TIK
SHE KNEW YOU. WHY DID AINE RECOGNIZE YOU?
WE'LL GET TO THAT LATER, CAPTAIN.

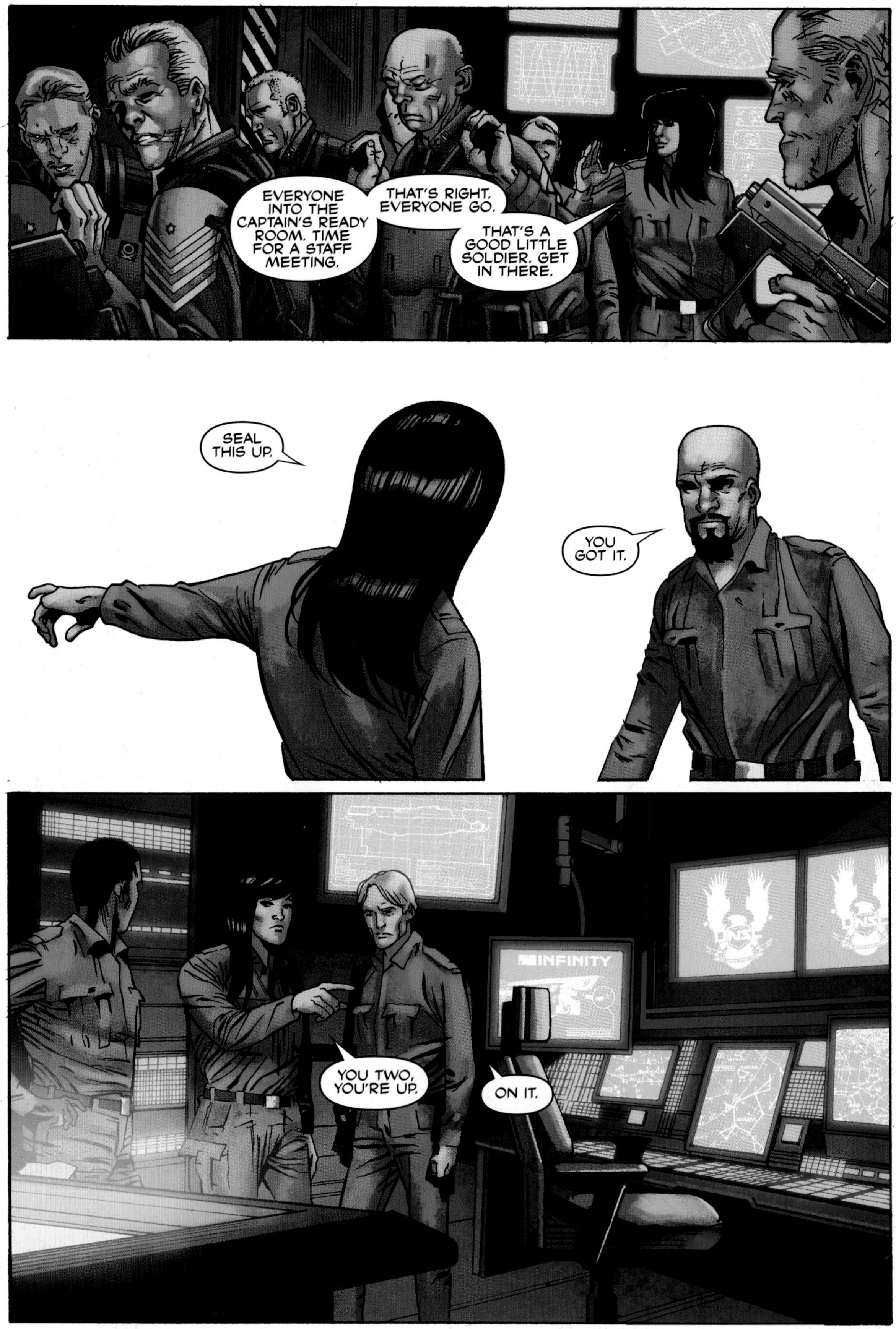
EVERYONE INTO THE CAPTAIN'S READY ROOM. TIME FOR A STAFF MEETING.
THAT'S RIGHT. EVERYONE GO.
THAT'S A GOOD LITTLE SOLDIER. GET IN THERE.
SEAL THIS UP.
YOU GOT IT.
INFINITY
YOU TWO, YOU'RE UP.
ON IT.

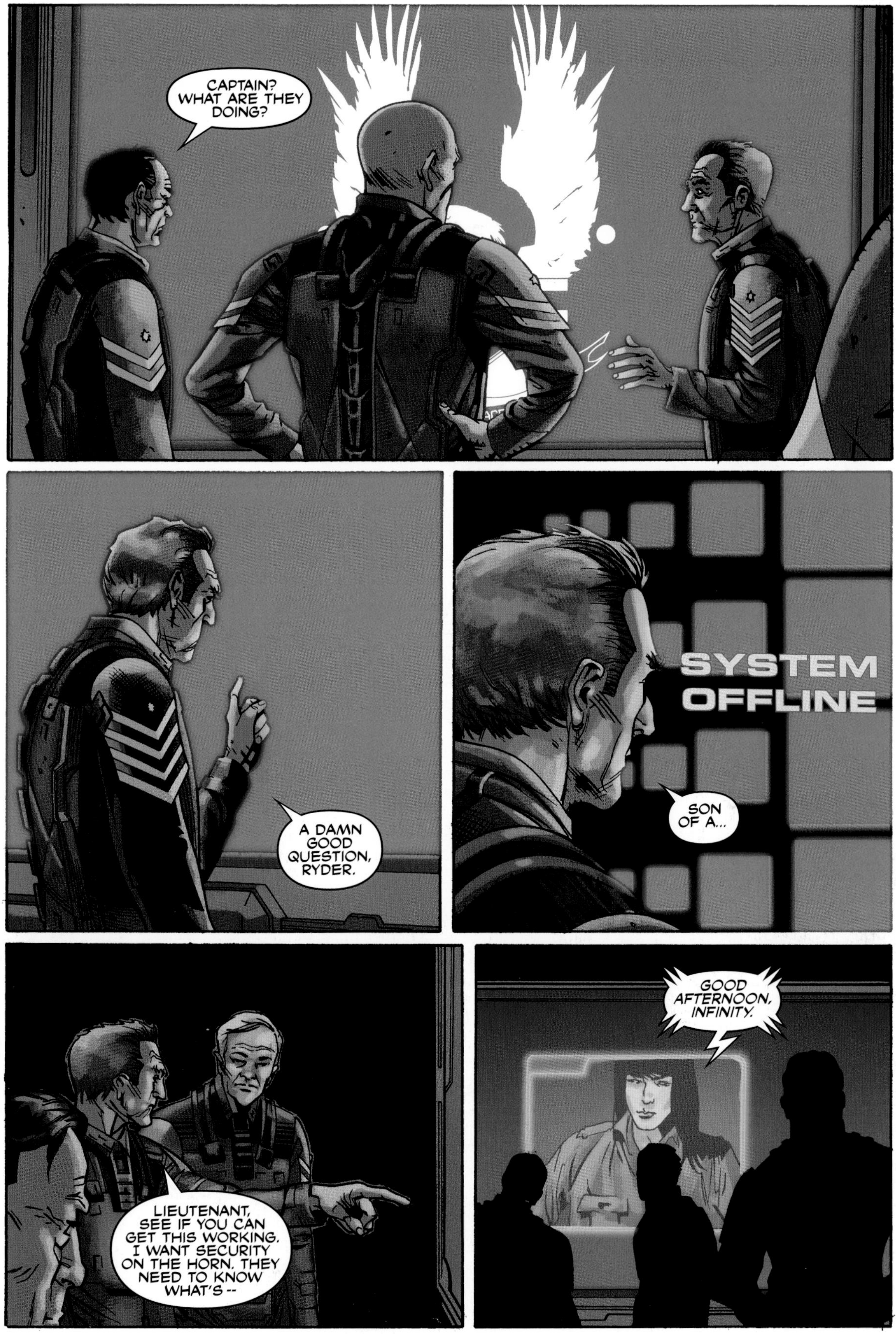
CAPTAIN? WHAT ARE THEY DOING?
A DAMN GOOD QUESTION, RYDER.
SYSTEM OFFLINE
SON OF A...
LIEUTENANT, SEE IF YOU CAN GET THIS WORKING. I WANT SECURITY ON THE HORN. THEY NEED TO KNOW WHAT'S --
GOOD AFTERNOON, INFINITY.

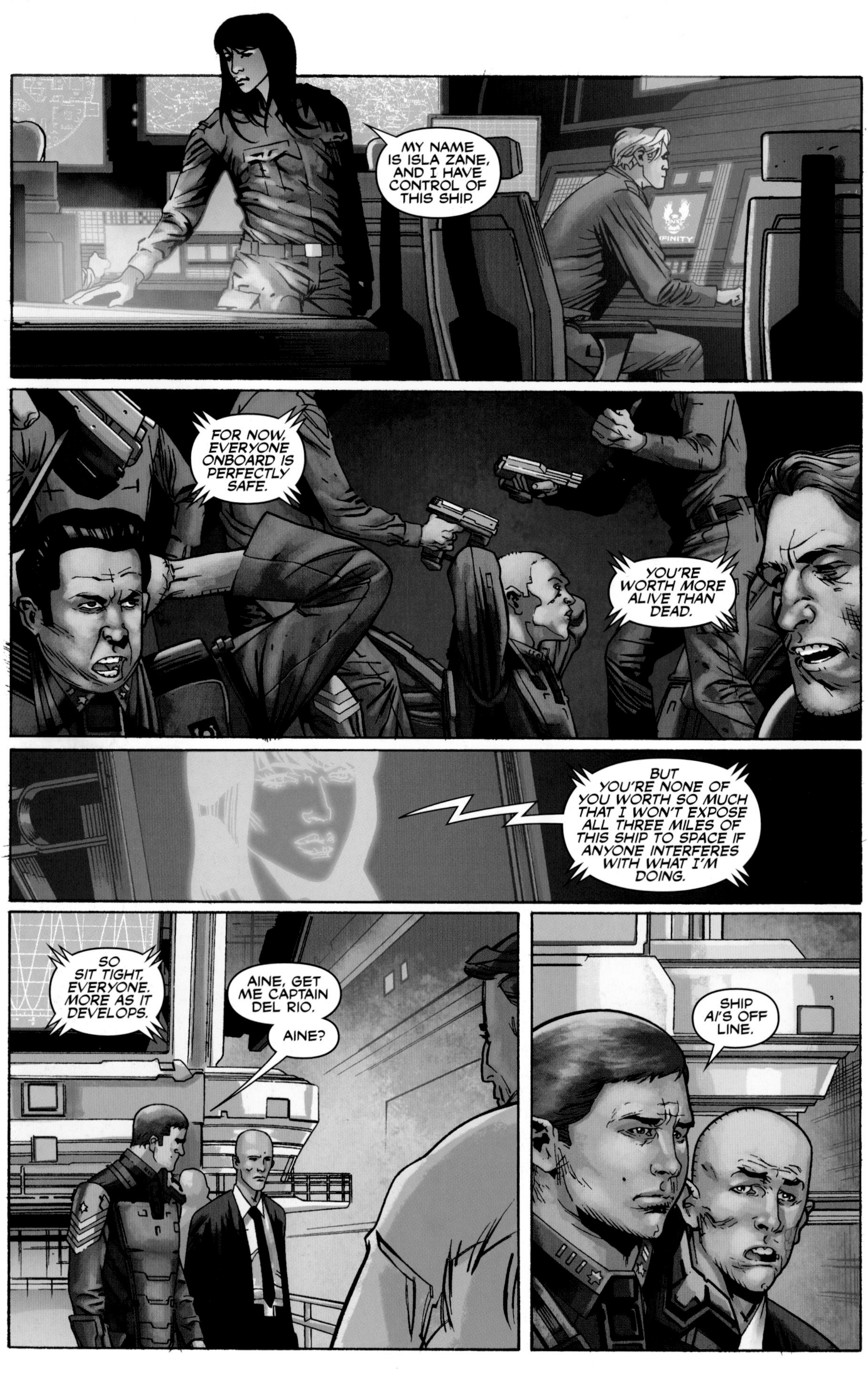
MY NAME IS ISLA ZANE, AND I HAVE CONTROL OF THIS SHIP.
INFINITY
FOR NOW, EVERYONE ONBOARD IS PERFECTLY SAFE.
YOU'RE WORTH MORE ALIVE THAN DEAD.
BUT YOU'RE NONE OF YOU WORTH SO MUCH THAT I WON'T EXPOSE ALL THREE MILES OF THIS SHIP TO SPACE IF ANYONE INTERFERES WITH WHAT I'M DOING.
SO SIT TIGHT, EVERYONE. MORE AS IT DEVELOPS.
AINE, GET ME CAPTAIN DEL RIO.
AINE?
SHIP AI'S OFF LINE.

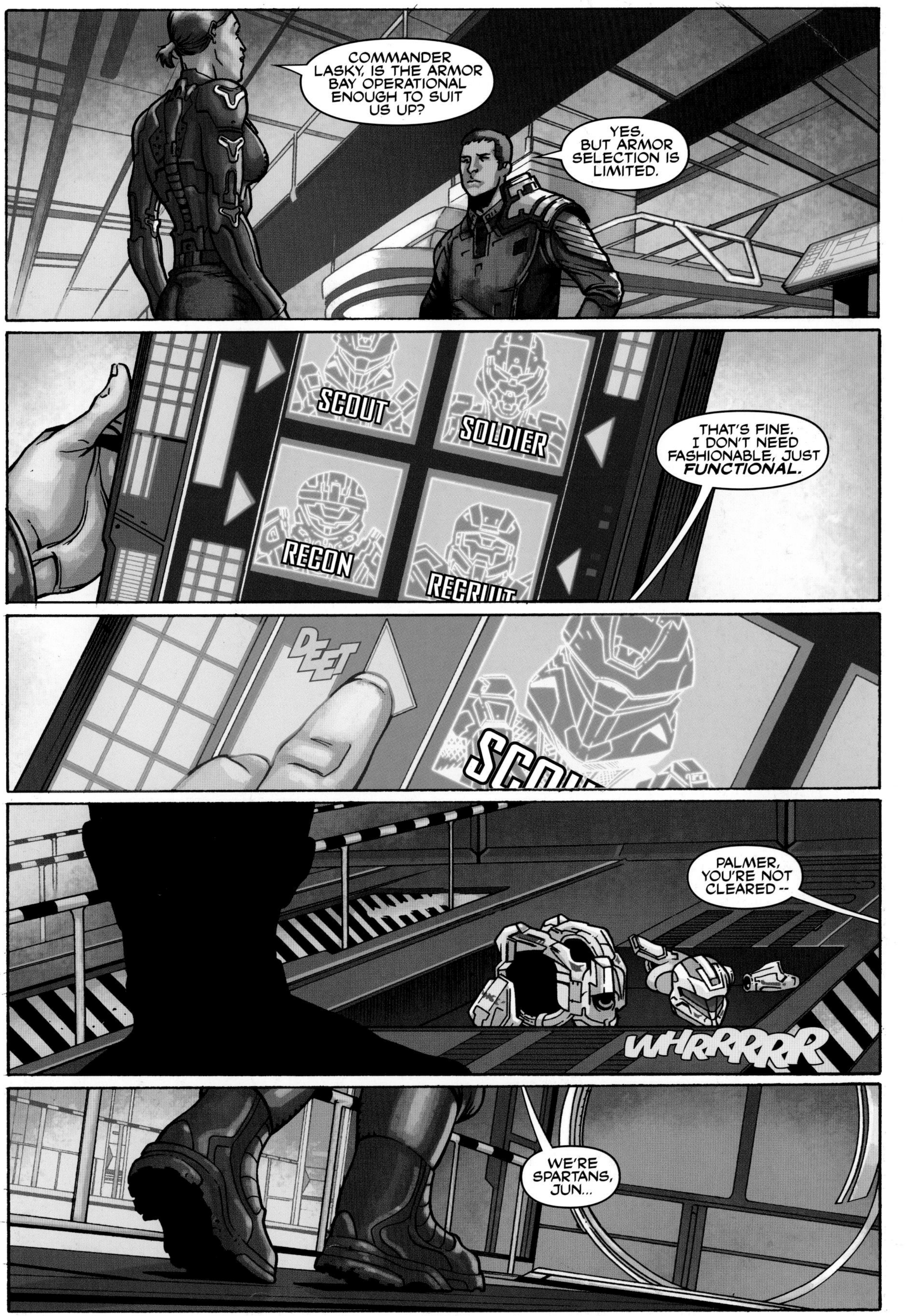
COMMANDER LASKY, IS THE ARMOR BAY OPERATIONAL ENOUGH TO SUIT US UP?
YES. BUT ARMOR SELECTION IS LIMITED.
SCOUT
SOLDIER
RECON
THAT'S FINE. I DON'T NEED FASHIONABLE, JUST *FUNCTIONAL.*
DEET
PALMER, YOU'RE NOT CLEARED --
WHRRRRR
WE'RE SPARTANS, JUN...

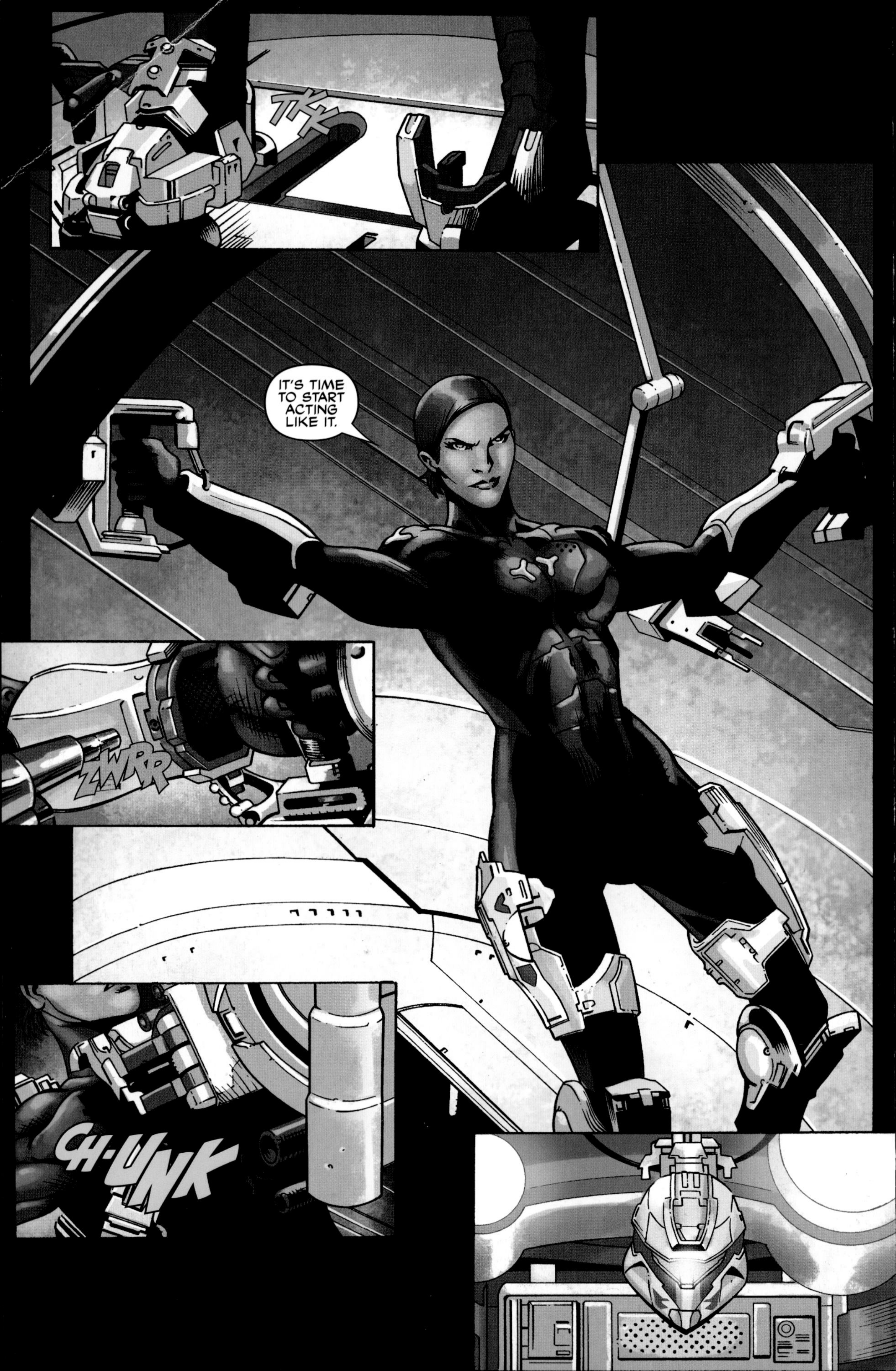
TKK
IT'S TIME TO START ACTING LIKE IT.
ZWRR
CH-UNK

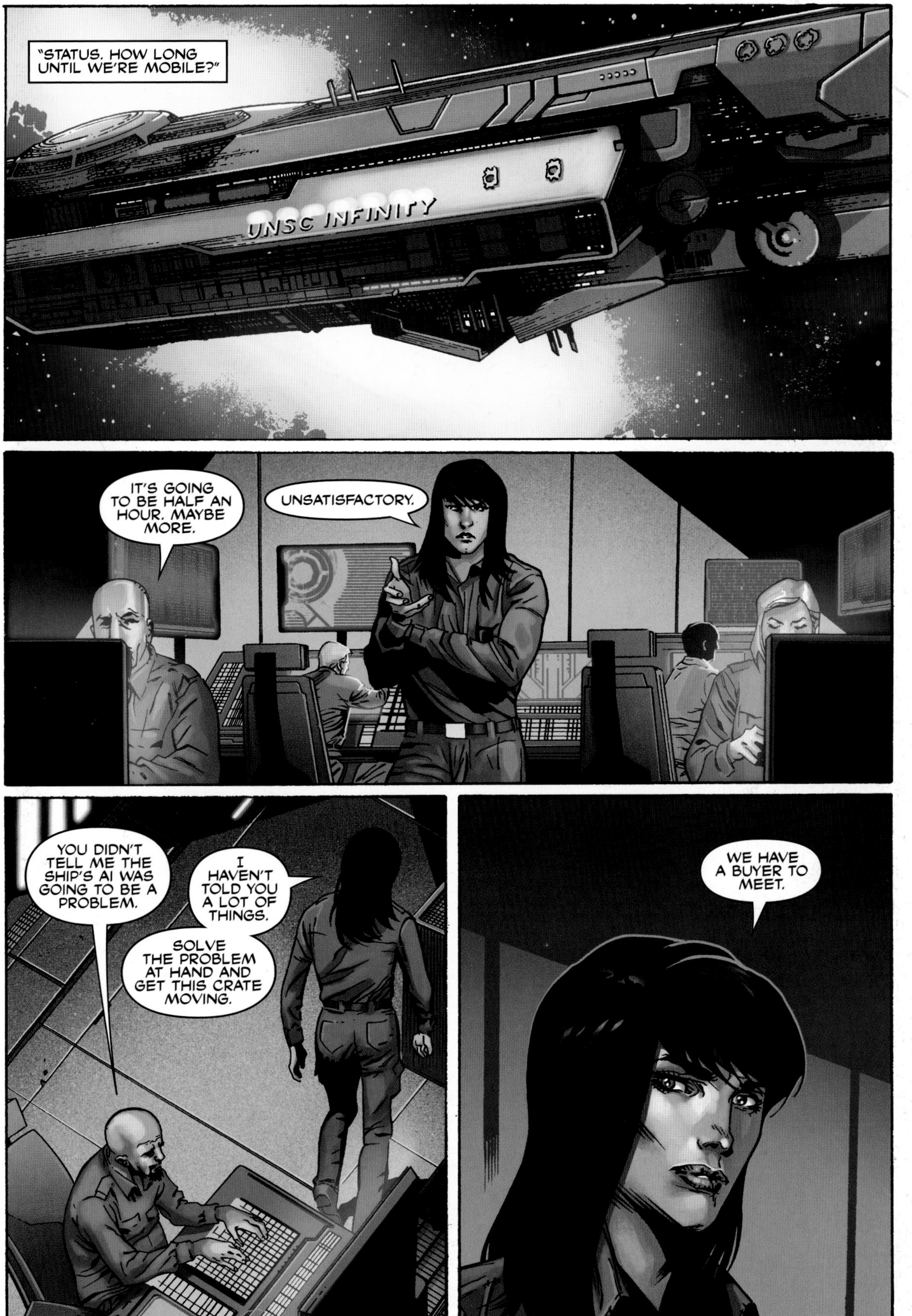
"STATUS. HOW LONG UNTIL WE'RE MOBILE?"
UNSC INFINITY
IT'S GOING TO BE HALF AN HOUR, MAYBE MORE.
UNSATISFACTORY.
YOU DIDN'T TELL ME THE SHIP'S AI WAS GOING TO BE A PROBLEM.
I HAVEN'T TOLD YOU A LOT OF THINGS.
SOLVE THE PROBLEM AT HAND AND GET THIS CRATE MOVING.
WE HAVE A BUYER TO MEET.

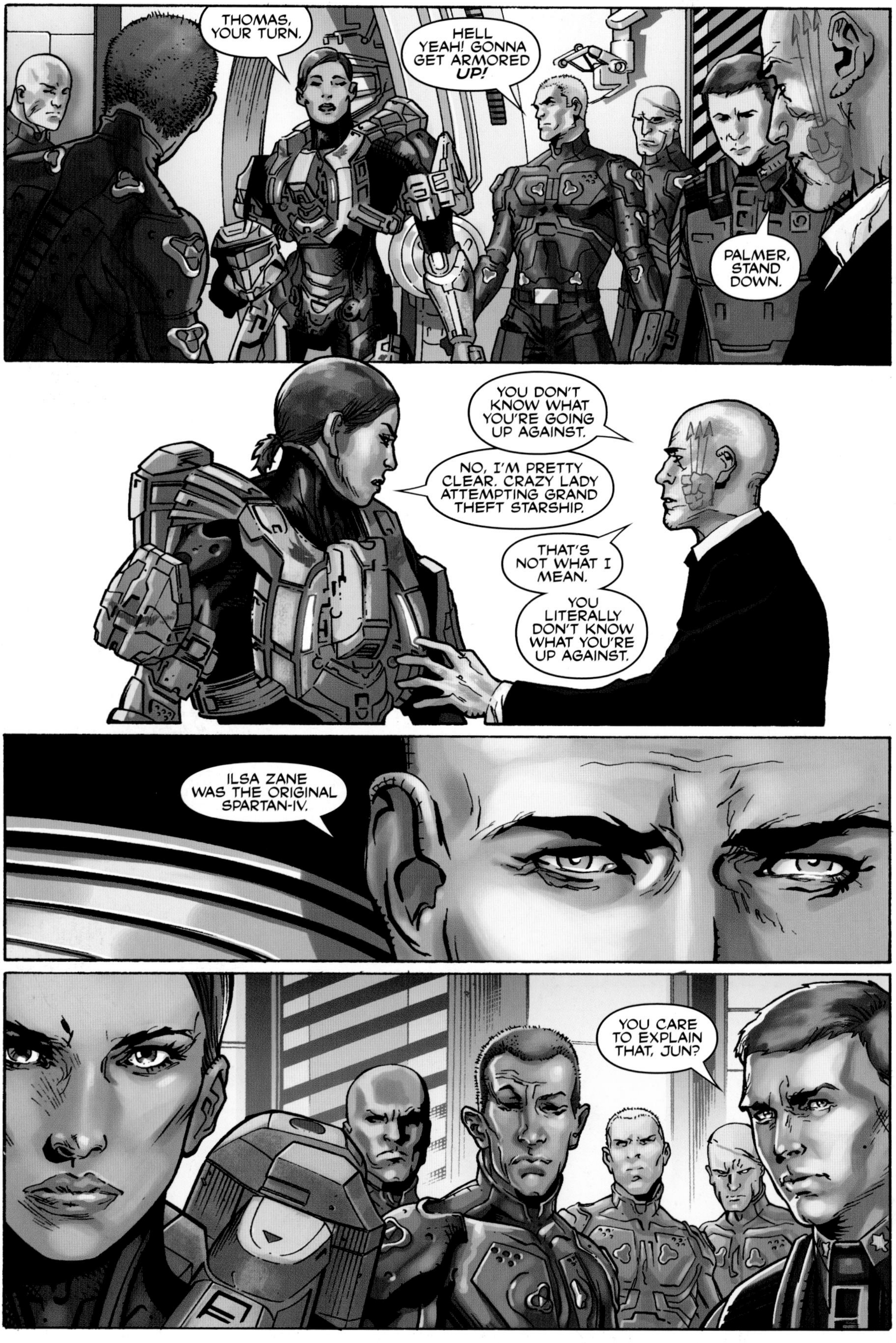
THOMAS, YOUR TURN.
HELL YEAH! GONNA GET ARMORED UP!
PALMER, STAND DOWN.
YOU DON'T KNOW WHAT YOU'RE GOING UP AGAINST.
NO, I'M PRETTY CLEAR. CRAZY LADY ATTEMPTING GRAND THEFT STARSHIP.
THAT'S NOT WHAT I MEAN.
YOU LITERALLY DON'T KNOW WHAT YOU'RE UP AGAINST.
ILSA ZANE WAS THE ORIGINAL SPARTAN-IV.
YOU CARE TO EXPLAIN THAT, JUN?

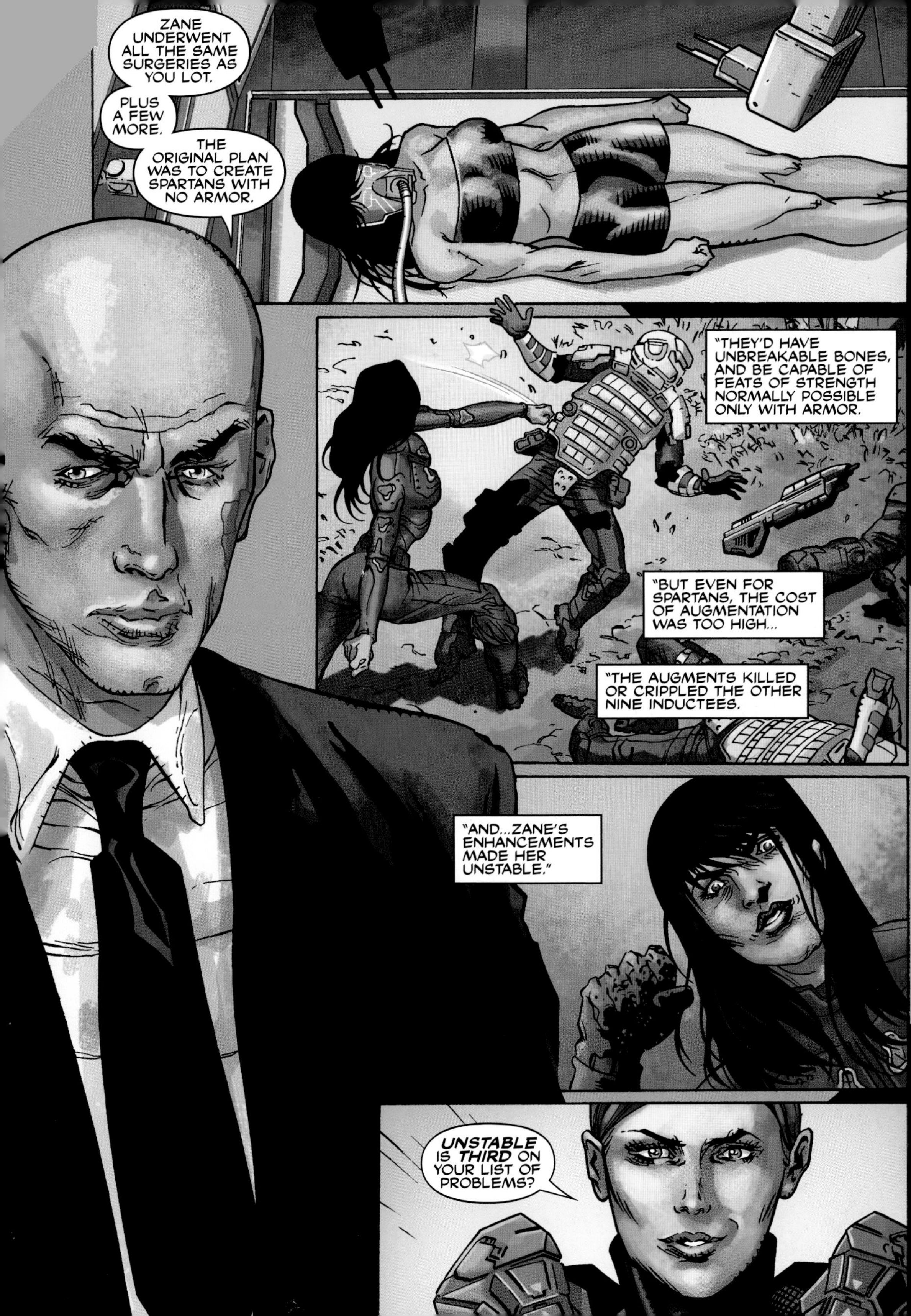
ZANE UNDERWENT ALL THE SAME SURGERIES AS YOU LOT.
PLUS A FEW MORE.
THE ORIGINAL PLAN WAS TO CREATE SPARTANS WITH NO ARMOR.
"THEY'D HAVE UNBREAKABLE BONES, AND BE CAPABLE OF FEATS OF STRENGTH NORMALLY POSSIBLE ONLY WITH ARMOR.
"BUT EVEN FOR SPARTANS, THE COST OF AUGMENTATION WAS TOO HIGH...
"THE AUGMENTS KILLED OR CRIPPLED THE OTHER NINE INDUCTEES.
"AND...ZANE'S ENHANCEMENTS MADE HER UNSTABLE."
UNSTABLE IS THIRD ON YOUR LIST OF PROBLEMS?

LAST I KNEW SHE WAS OUT OF SPARTANS AND INTO THE *OFFICE OF NAVAL INTELLIGENCE.*

SHE WAS TOO UNSTABLE TO BE A SPARTAN, BUT NOT ONI?

SOMETIMES, SPARTAN DAVIS, YOU NEED UNSTABLE TO GET THE JOB DONE.

WHAT THE HELL? I GET CRAP FOR SAYING THINGS LIKE THAT.

I NEED TO GET TO A WORKING SECURITY CONSOLE. MAYBE WE CAN FIND OUT WHAT'S GOING ON.

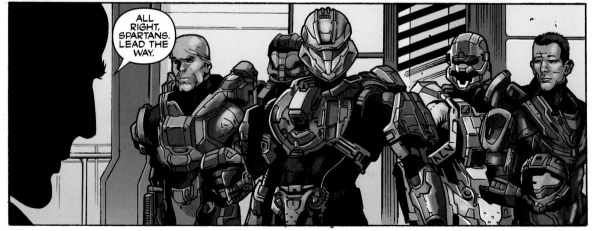

ALL RIGHT, SPARTANS. LEAD THE WAY.

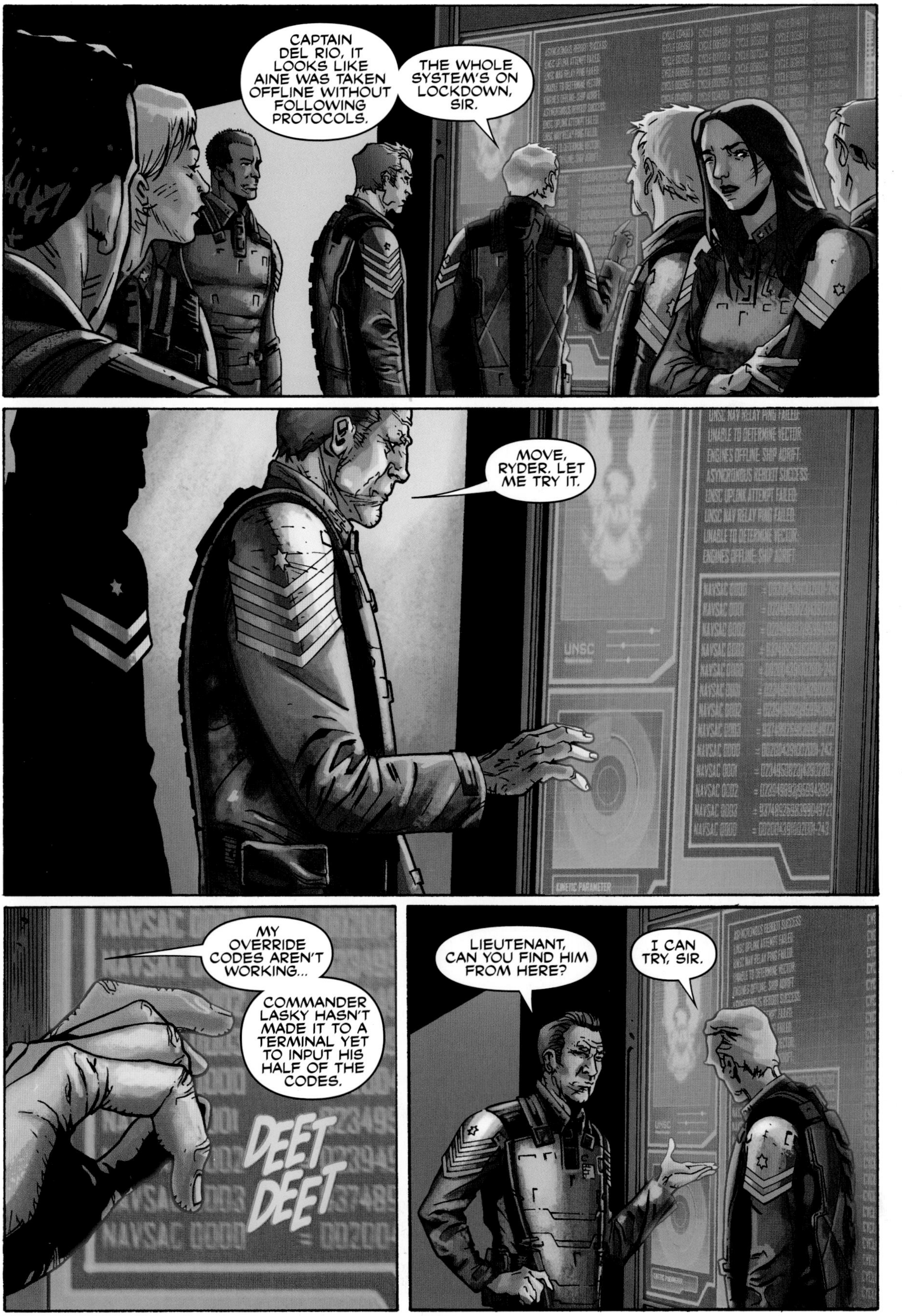
CAPTAIN DEL RIO, IT LOOKS LIKE AINE WAS TAKEN OFFLINE WITHOUT FOLLOWING PROTOCOLS.
THE WHOLE SYSTEM'S ON LOCKDOWN, SIR.
MOVE, RYDER. LET ME TRY IT.
MY OVERRIDE CODES AREN'T WORKING...
COMMANDER LASKY HASN'T MADE IT TO A TERMINAL YET TO INPUT HIS HALF OF THE CODES.
DEET DEET
LIEUTENANT, CAN YOU FIND HIM FROM HERE?
I CAN TRY, SIR.

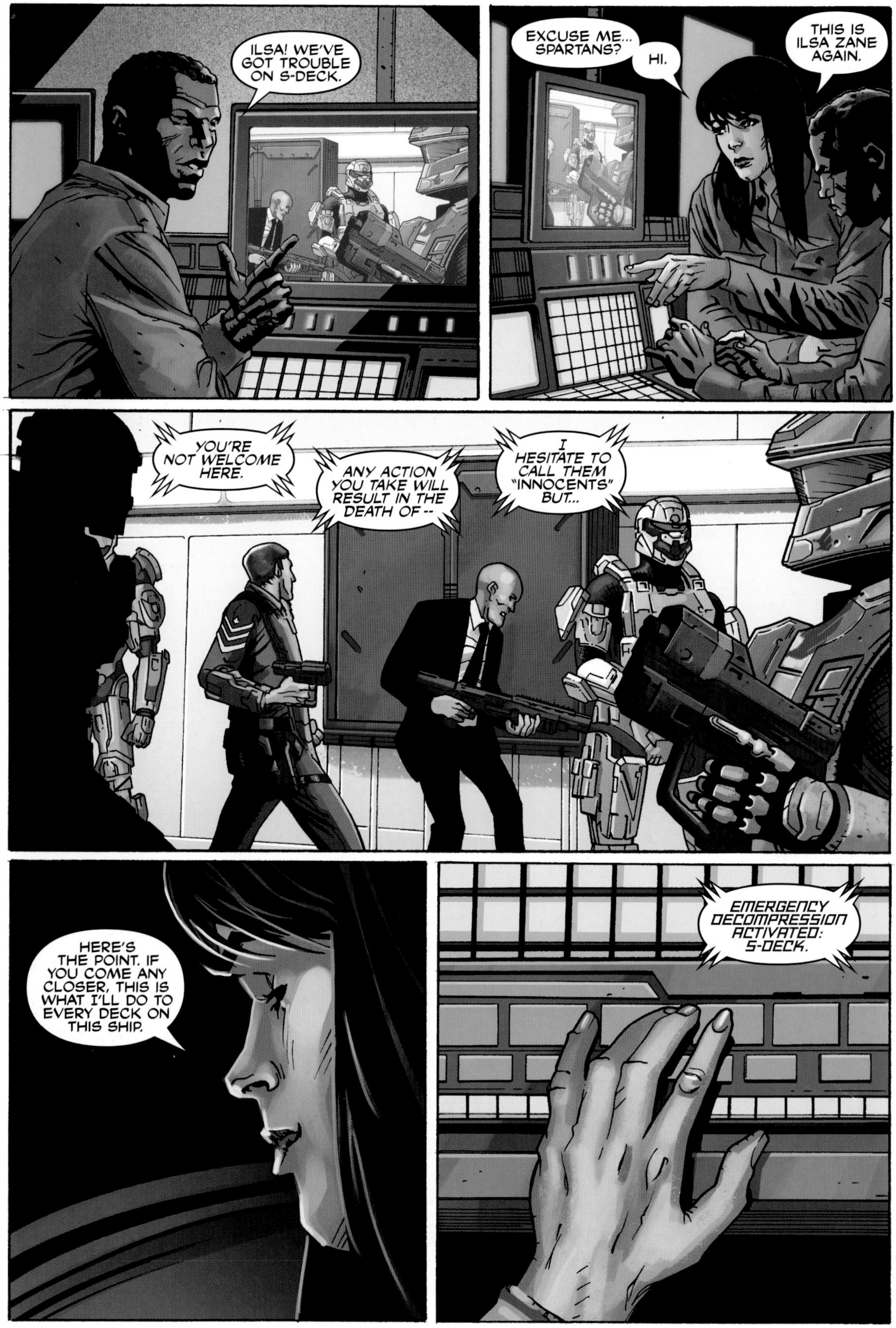
ILSA! WE'VE GOT TROUBLE ON S-DECK.
EXCUSE ME... SPARTANS?
HI.
THIS IS ILSA ZANE AGAIN.
YOU'RE NOT WELCOME HERE.
ANY ACTION YOU TAKE WILL RESULT IN THE DEATH OF --
I HESITATE TO CALL THEM "INNOCENTS" BUT...
HERE'S THE POINT. IF YOU COME ANY CLOSER, THIS IS WHAT I'LL DO TO EVERY DECK ON THIS SHIP.
EMERGENCY DECOMPRESSION ACTIVATED: S-DECK.

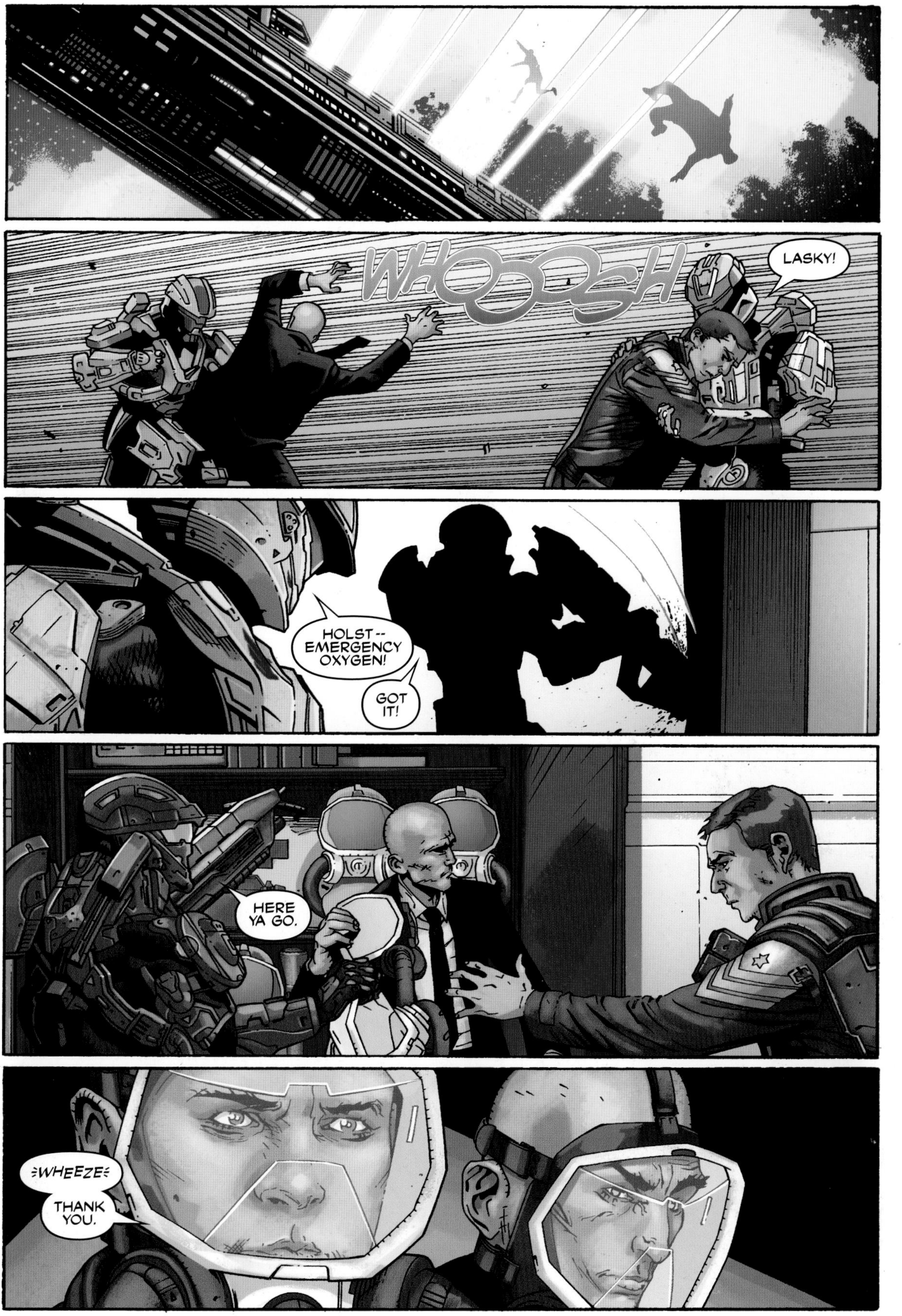
WHOOOOSH
LASKY!
HOLST -- EMERGENCY OXYGEN!
GOT IT!
HERE YA GO.
WHEEZE
THANK YOU.

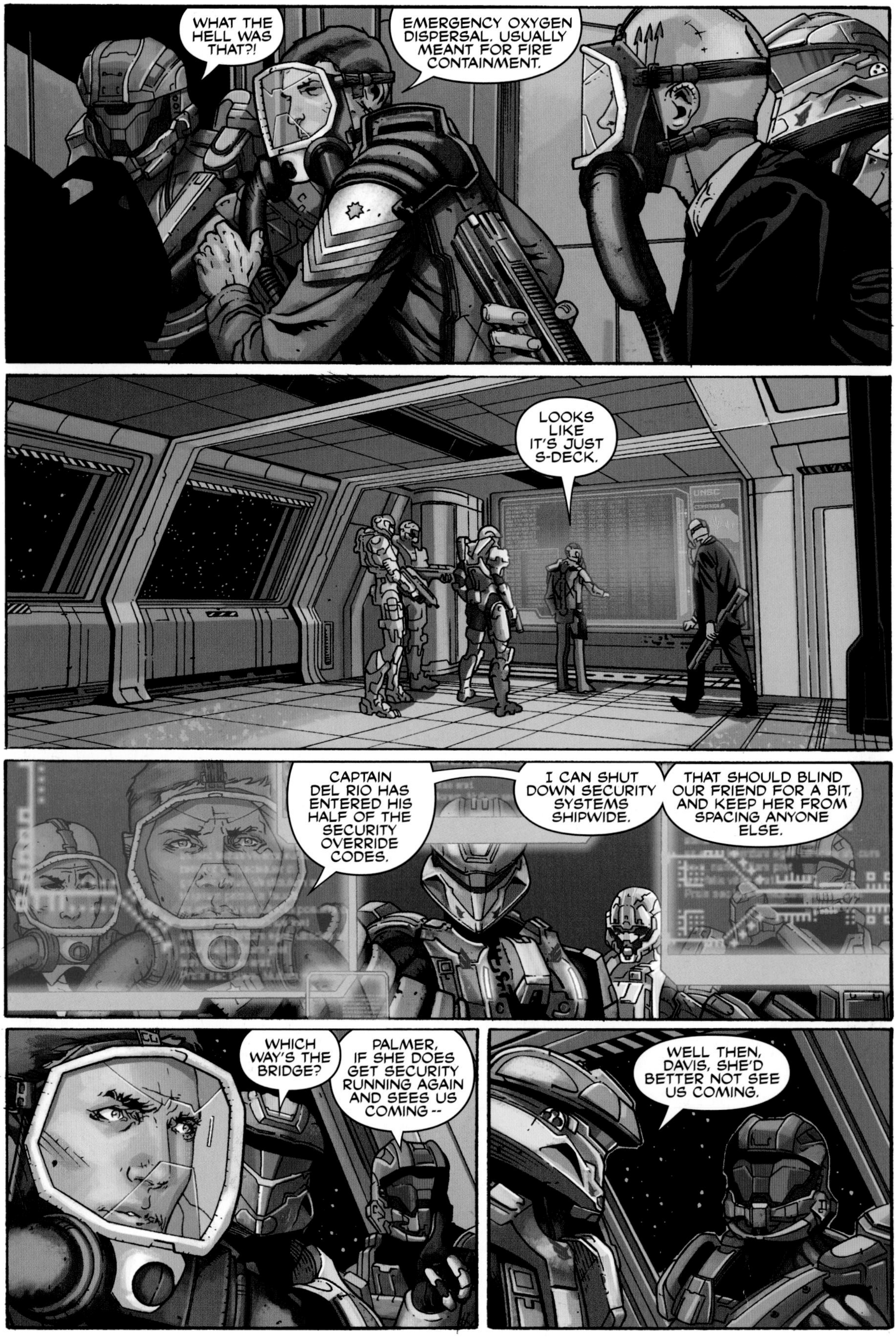
WHAT THE HELL WAS THAT?!
EMERGENCY OXYGEN DISPERSAL. USUALLY MEANT FOR FIRE CONTAINMENT.
LOOKS LIKE IT'S JUST S-DECK.
CAPTAIN DEL RIO HAS ENTERED HIS HALF OF THE SECURITY OVERRIDE CODES.
I CAN SHUT DOWN SECURITY SYSTEMS SHIPWIDE.
THAT SHOULD BLIND OUR FRIEND FOR A BIT, AND KEEP HER FROM SPACING ANYONE ELSE.
WHICH WAY'S THE BRIDGE?
PALMER, IF SHE DOES GET SECURITY RUNNING AGAIN AND SEES US COMING --
WELL THEN, DAVIS, SHE'D BETTER NOT SEE US COMING.

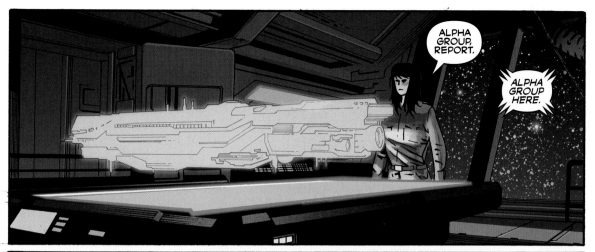

ALPHA GROUP, REPORT.

ALPHA GROUP HERE.

SWEEP S-DECK. IF THE SPARTANS ARE STILL THERE, ELIMINATE THEM.

UNDERSTOOD. WHAT ABOUT CREW MEMBERS?

THE *BUYER* EXPRESSED INTEREST IN ANY COMMAND CREW WE CAN KEEP ALIVE.

SPEAKING OF WHICH... PROBABLY TIME TO GET ADMIRAL DRAKE ON THE HORN.

SIR, THERE'S SOMEONE USING A SECURITY PANEL ON S-DECK.

APPEARS TO BE COMMANDER LASKY'S OVERRIDE CODES.

CAN YOU TALK TO HIM?

I THINK SO--

LIEUTENANT RYDER?

OUT OF MY WAY, RYDER!

LASKY! THERE'S BEEN A SECURITY BREACH!

I'M AWARE, SIR.

WE'VE GOT FIVE SPARTANS ON THIS SHIP--

THREE NOW, SIR. WE ONLY HAVE THREE.

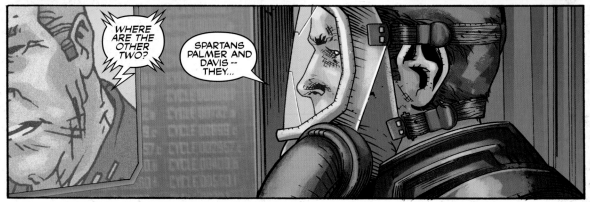

WHERE ARE THE OTHER TWO?

SPARTANS PALMER AND DAVIS-- THEY...

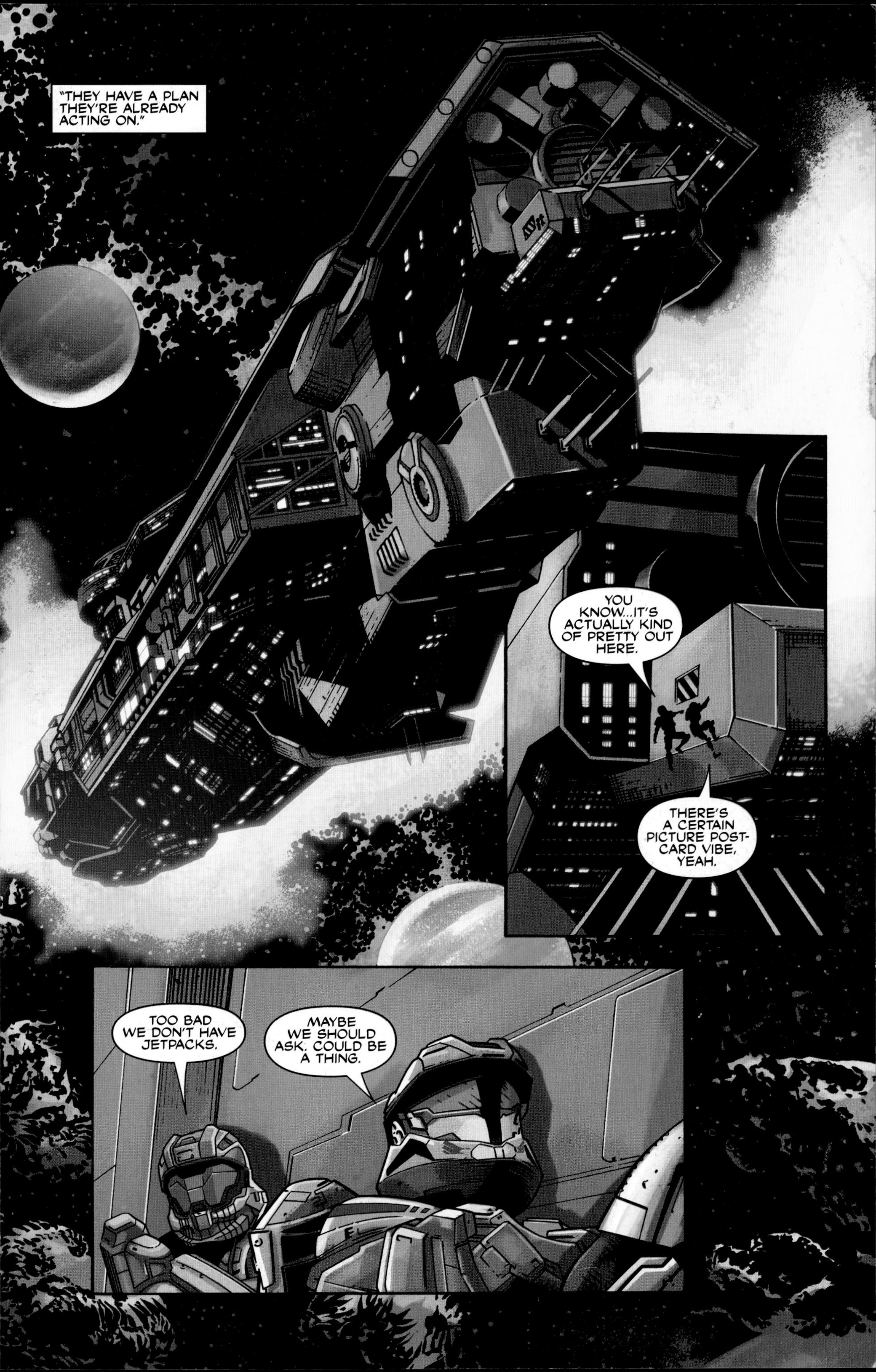
"THEY HAVE A PLAN THEY'RE ALREADY ACTING ON."
YOU KNOW...IT'S ACTUALLY KIND OF PRETTY OUT HERE.
THERE'S A CERTAIN PICTURE POST-CARD VIBE, YEAH.
TOO BAD WE DON'T HAVE JETPACKS.
MAYBE WE SHOULD ASK. COULD BE A THING.

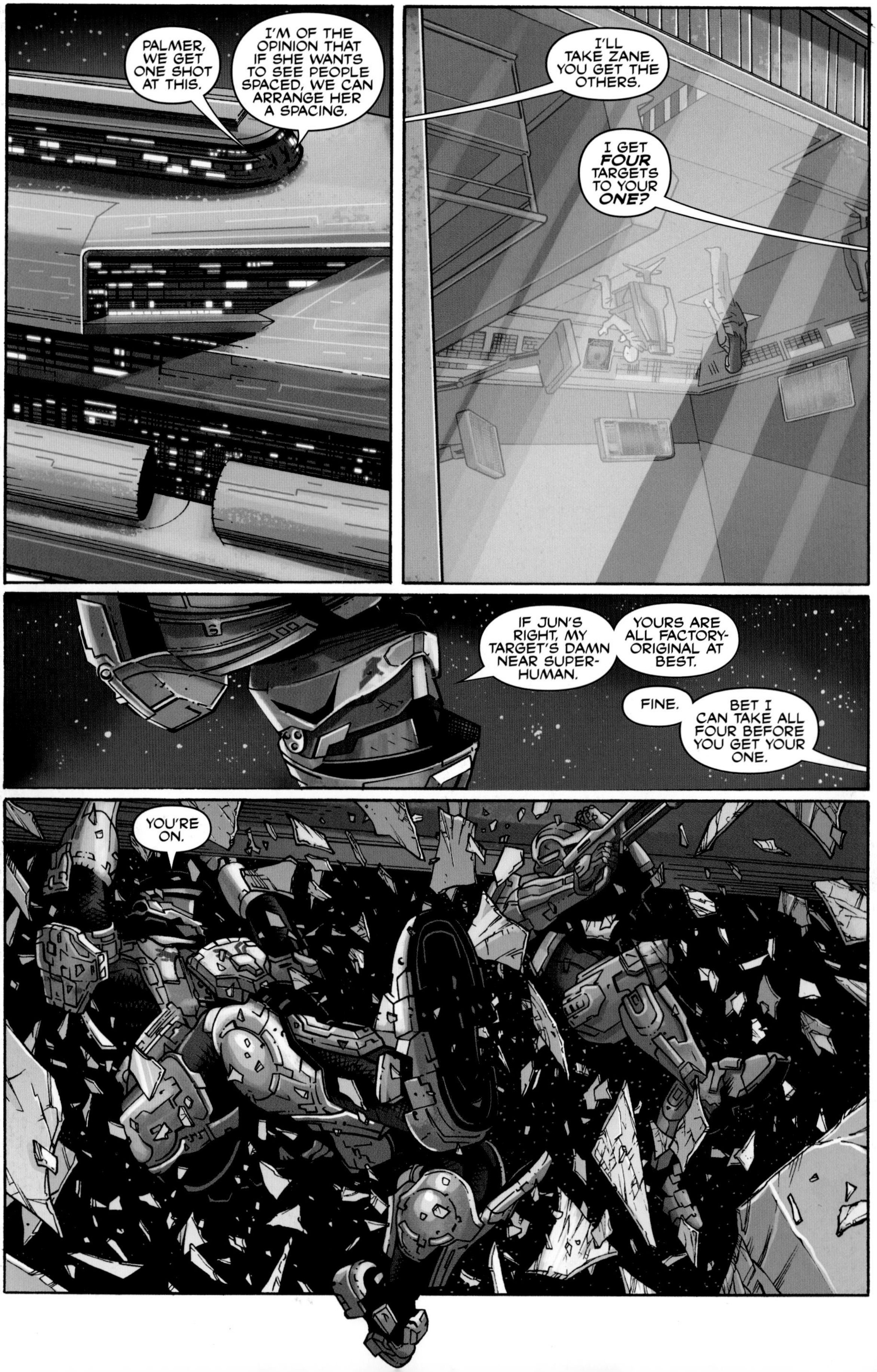
PALMER, WE GET ONE SHOT AT THIS.
I'M OF THE OPINION THAT IF SHE WANTS TO SEE PEOPLE SPACED, WE CAN ARRANGE HER A SPACING.
I'LL TAKE ZANE. YOU GET THE OTHERS.
I GET ***FOUR*** TARGETS TO YOUR ***ONE?***
IF JUN'S RIGHT, MY TARGET'S DAMN NEAR SUPER-HUMAN.
YOURS ARE ALL FACTORY-ORIGINAL AT BEST.
FINE.
BET I CAN TAKE ALL FOUR BEFORE YOU GET YOUR ONE.
YOU'RE ON.

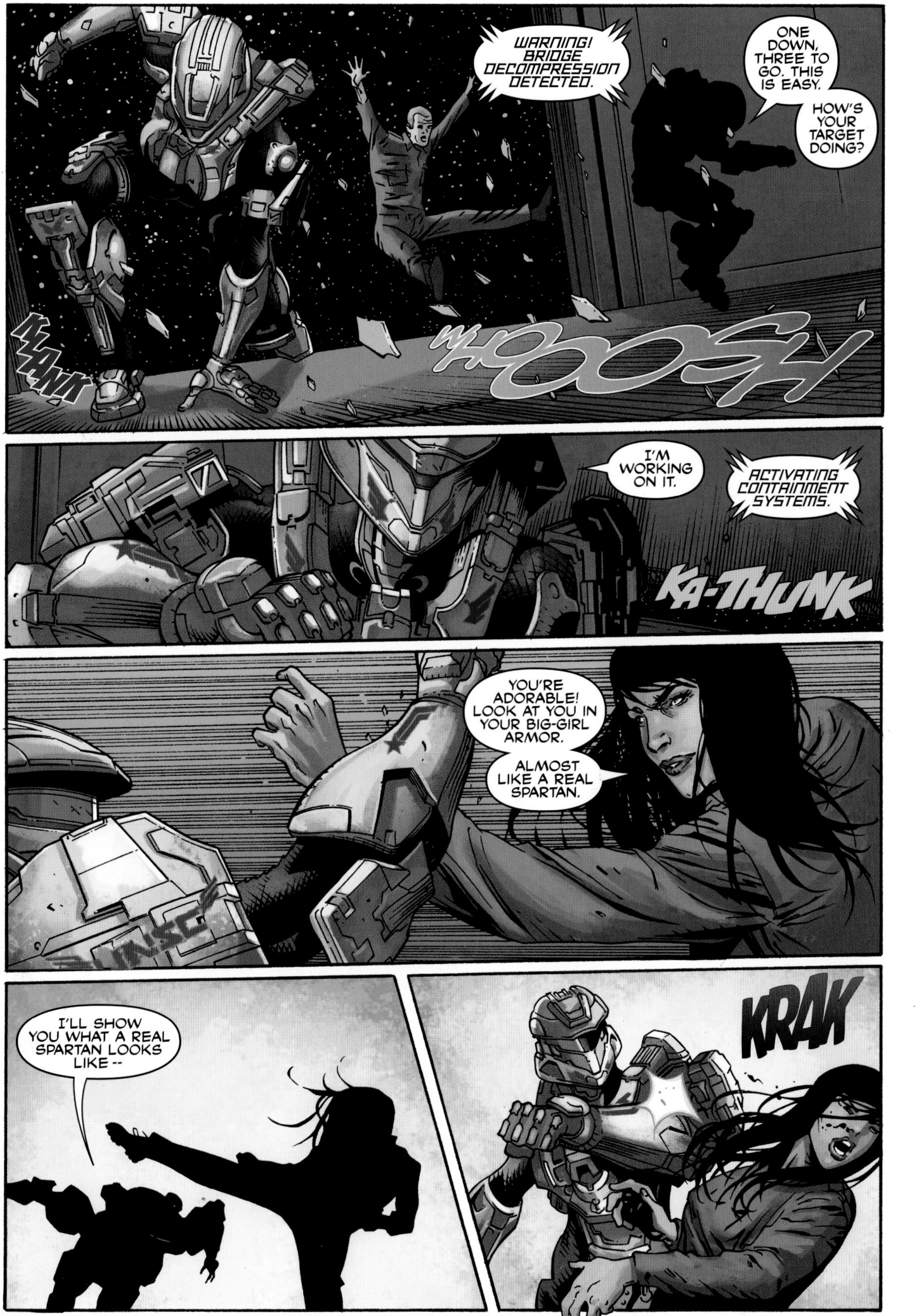
WARNING! BRIDGE DECOMPRESSION DETECTED.
ONE DOWN, THREE TO GO. THIS IS EASY.
HOW'S YOUR TARGET DOING?
WHOOSH
I'M WORKING ON IT.
ACTIVATING CONTAINMENT SYSTEMS.
KA-THUNK
YOU'RE ADORABLE! LOOK AT YOU IN YOUR BIG-GIRL ARMOR.
ALMOST LIKE A REAL SPARTAN.
I'LL SHOW YOU WHAT A REAL SPARTAN LOOKS LIKE --
KRAK

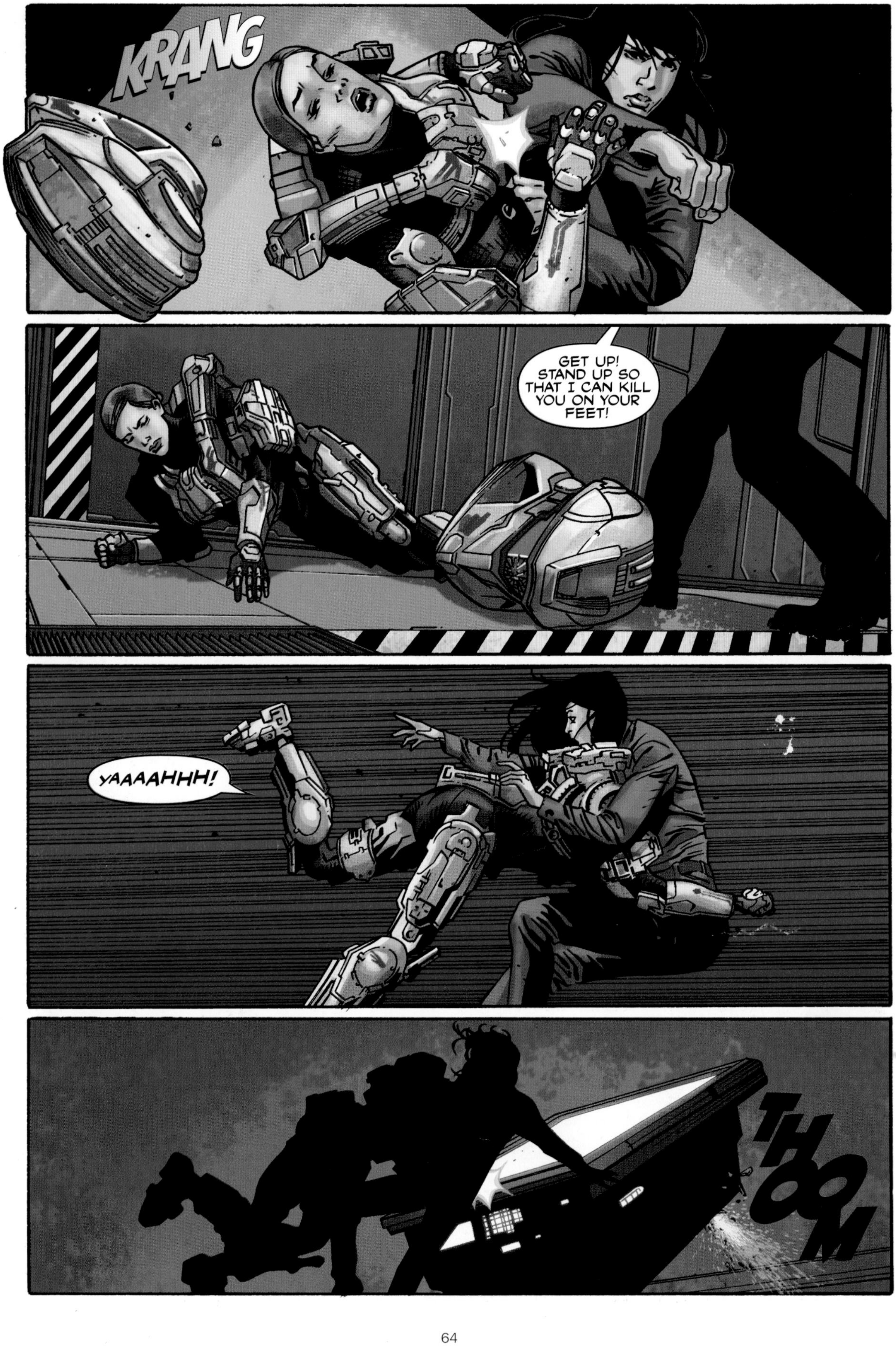
KRANG
GET UP! STAND UP SO THAT I CAN KILL YOU ON YOUR FEET!
YAAAAHHH!
THOOM

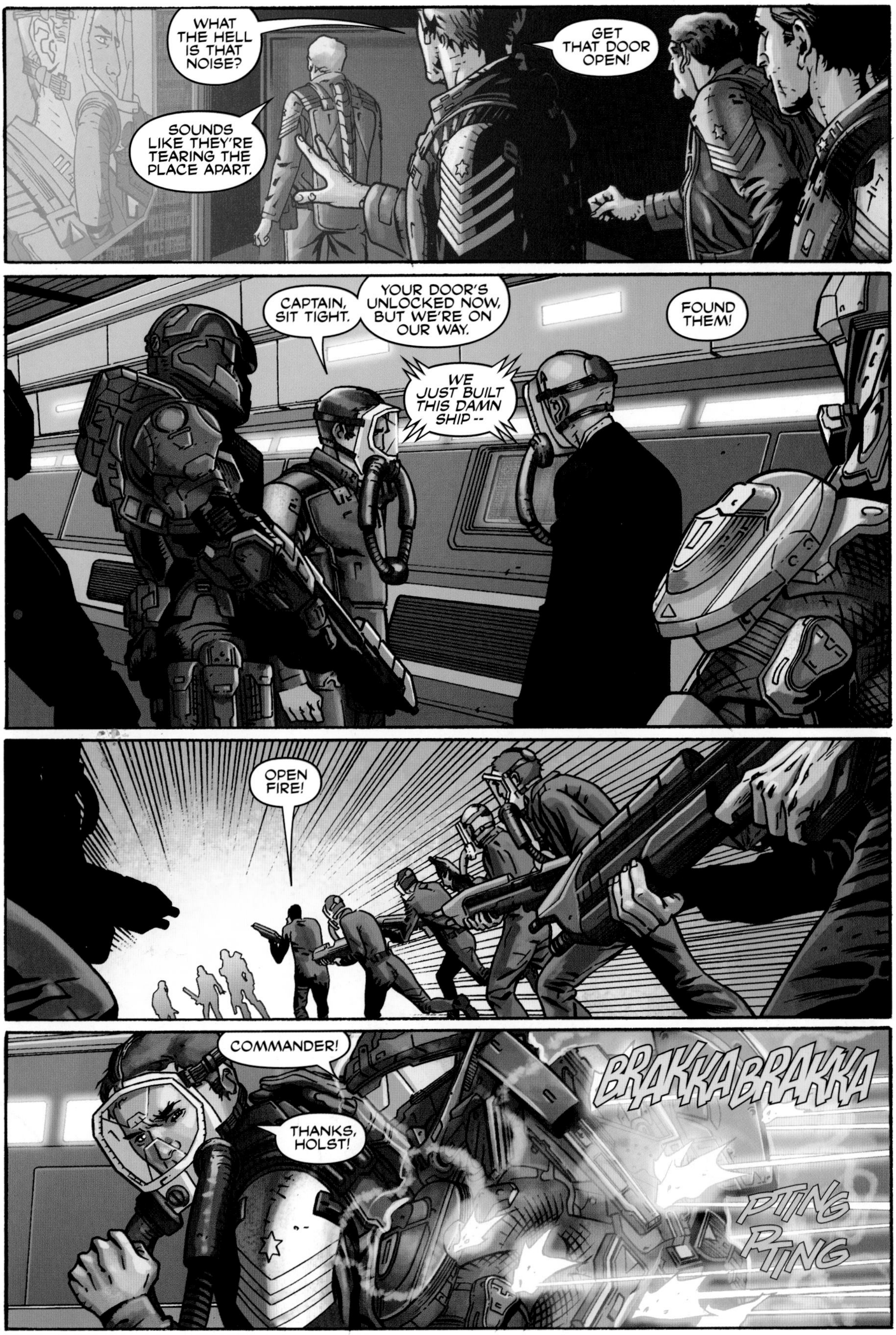
WHAT THE HELL IS THAT NOISE?
SOUNDS LIKE THEY'RE TEARING THE PLACE APART.
GET THAT DOOR OPEN!
CAPTAIN, SIT TIGHT.
YOUR DOOR'S UNLOCKED NOW, BUT WE'RE ON OUR WAY.
WE JUST BUILT THIS DAMN SHIP --
FOUND THEM!
OPEN FIRE!
COMMANDER!
THANKS, HOLST!
BRAKKA BRAKKA
PTING
PTING

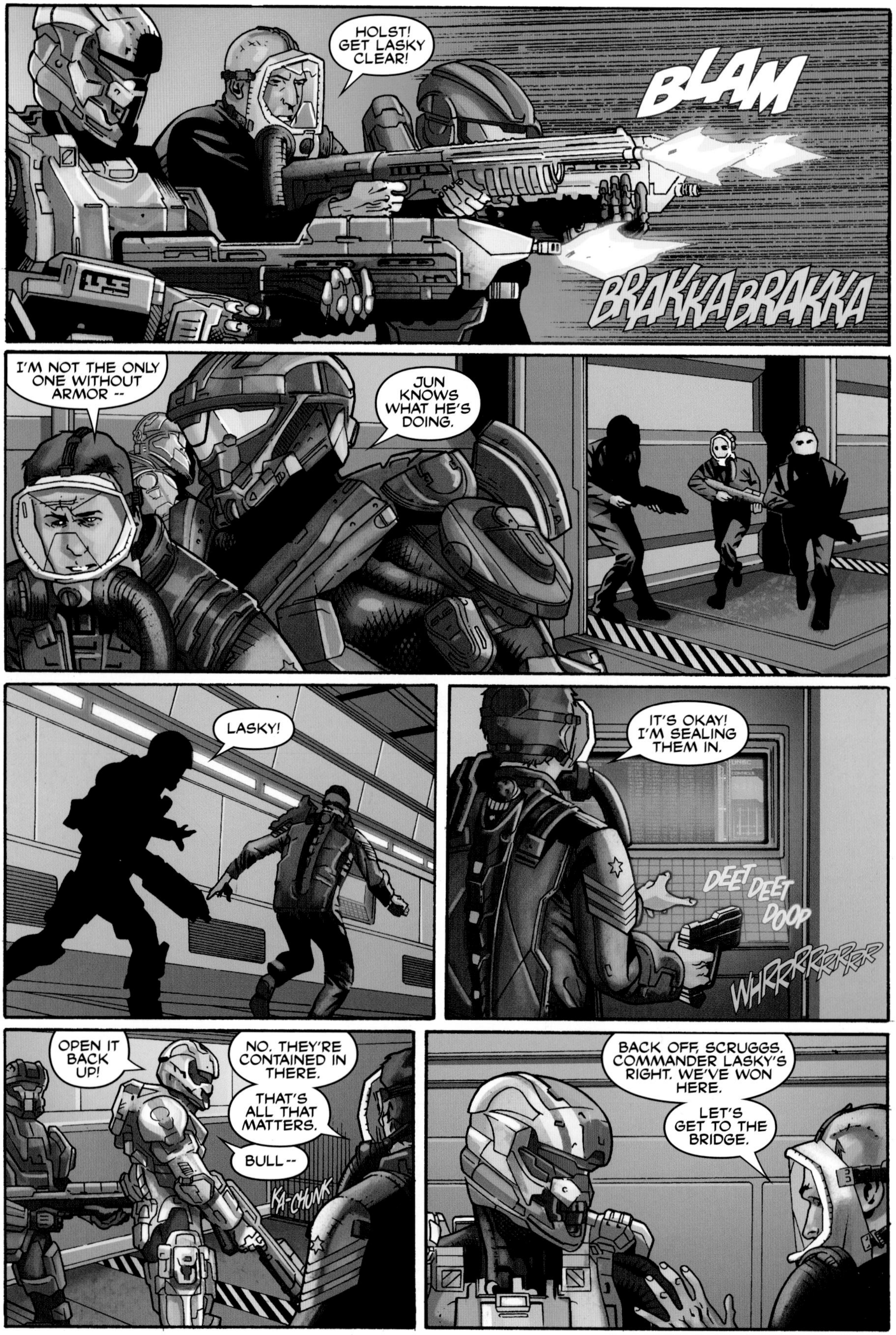
HOLST! GET LASKY CLEAR!
BLAM
BRAKKA BRAKKA
I'M NOT THE ONLY ONE WITHOUT ARMOR --
JUN KNOWS WHAT HE'S DOING.
LASKY!
IT'S OKAY! I'M SEALING THEM IN.
DEET DEET DOOP
WHRRRRRRRR
OPEN IT BACK UP!
NO. THEY'RE CONTAINED IN THERE.
THAT'S ALL THAT MATTERS.
BULL --
KA-CHUNK
BACK OFF, SCRUGGS. COMMANDER LASKY'S RIGHT. WE'VE WON HERE.
LET'S GET TO THE BRIDGE.

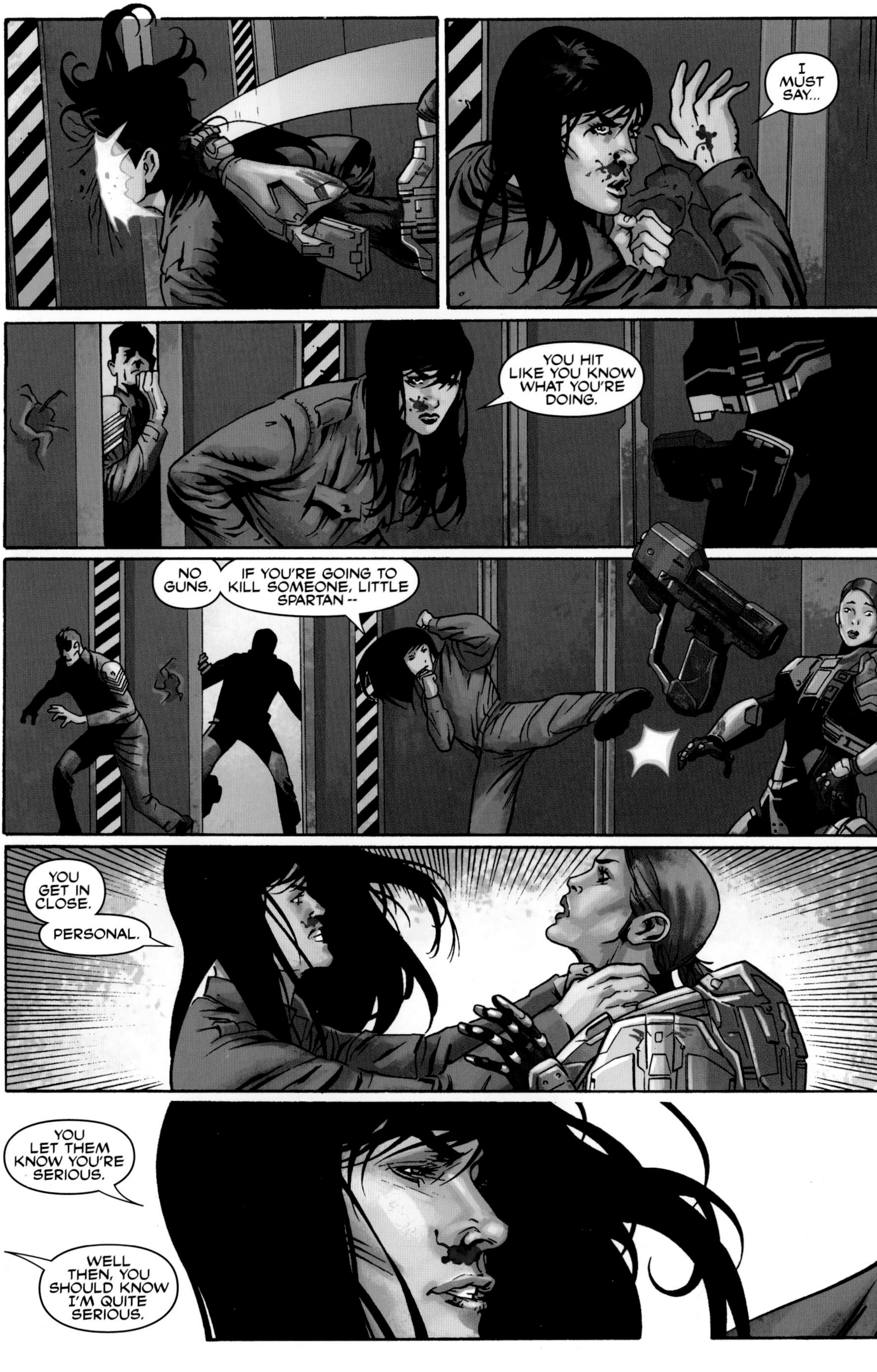
I MUST SAY...
YOU HIT LIKE YOU KNOW WHAT YOU'RE DOING.
NO GUNS.
IF YOU'RE GOING TO KILL SOMEONE, LITTLE SPARTAN --
YOU GET IN CLOSE.
PERSONAL.
YOU LET THEM KNOW YOU'RE SERIOUS.
WELL THEN, YOU SHOULD KNOW I'M QUITE SERIOUS.

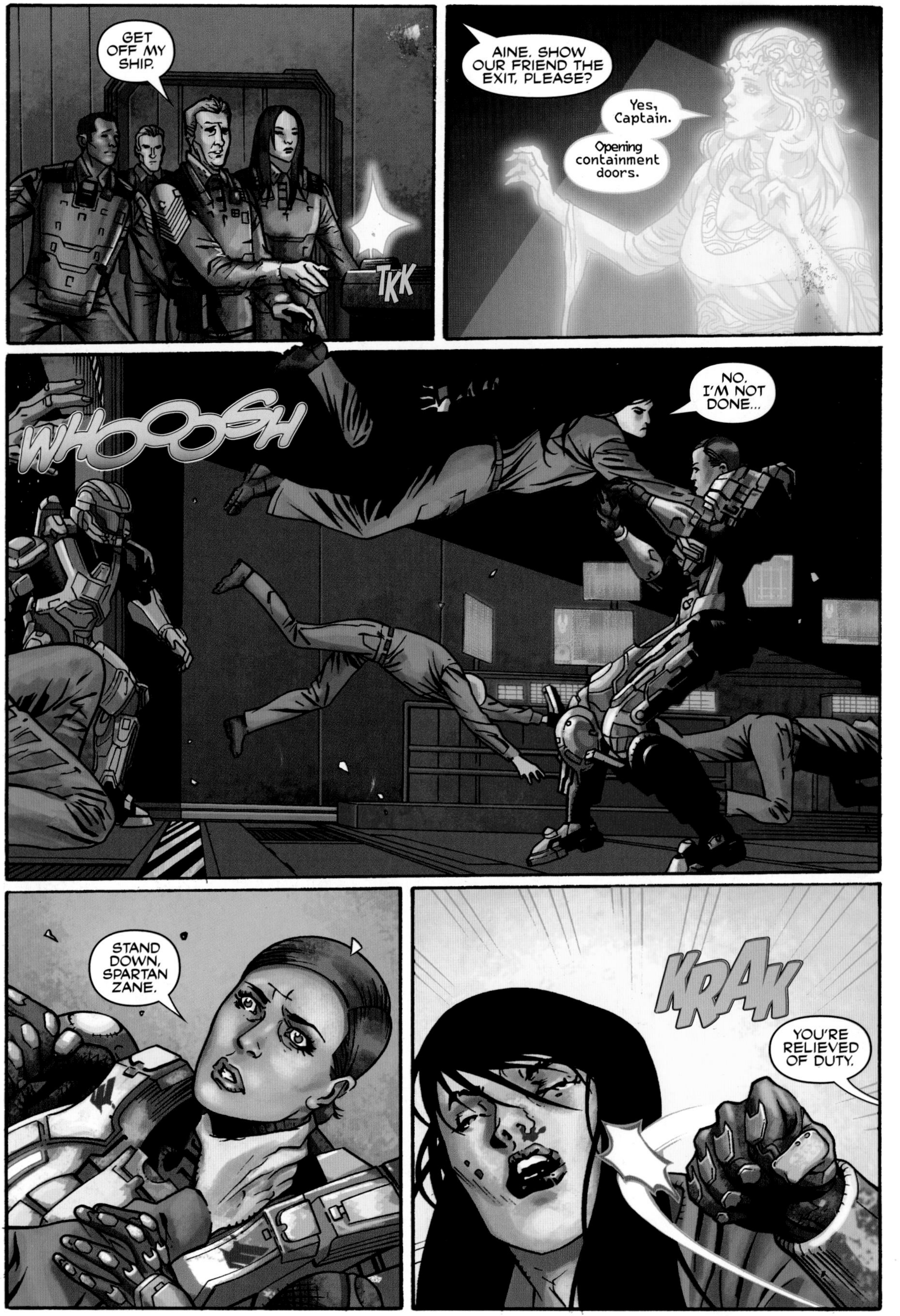
GET OFF MY SHIP.
TKK
AINE. SHOW OUR FRIEND THE EXIT, PLEASE?
Yes, Captain.
Opening containment doors.
WHOOOSH
NO. I'M NOT DONE...
STAND DOWN, SPARTAN ZANE.
KRAK
YOU'RE RELIEVED OF DUTY.

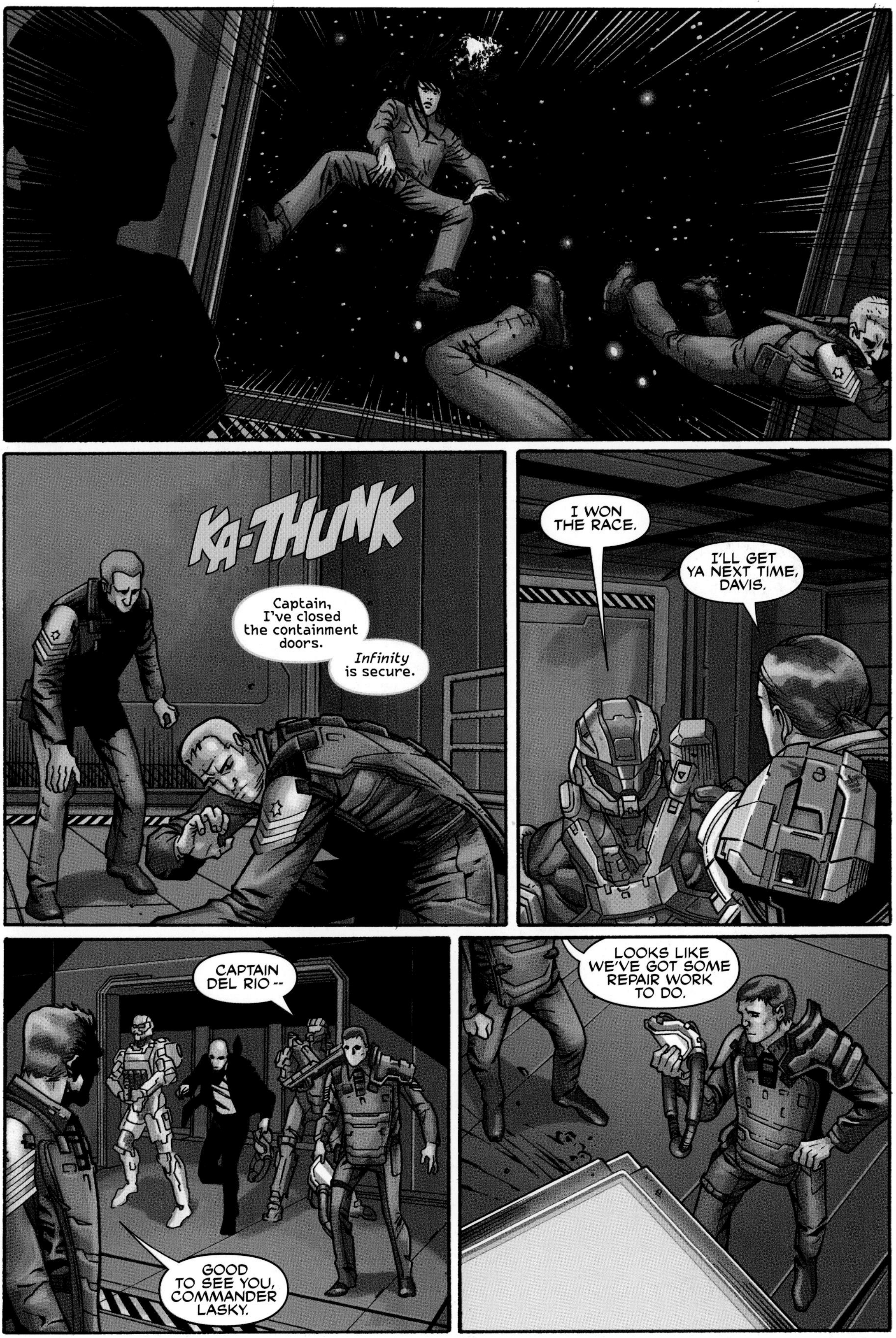
KA-THUNK
Captain, I've closed the containment doors.
Infinity is secure.
I WON THE RACE.
I'LL GET YA NEXT TIME, DAVIS.
CAPTAIN DEL RIO --
GOOD TO SEE YOU, COMMANDER LASKY.
LOOKS LIKE WE'VE GOT SOME REPAIR WORK TO DO.

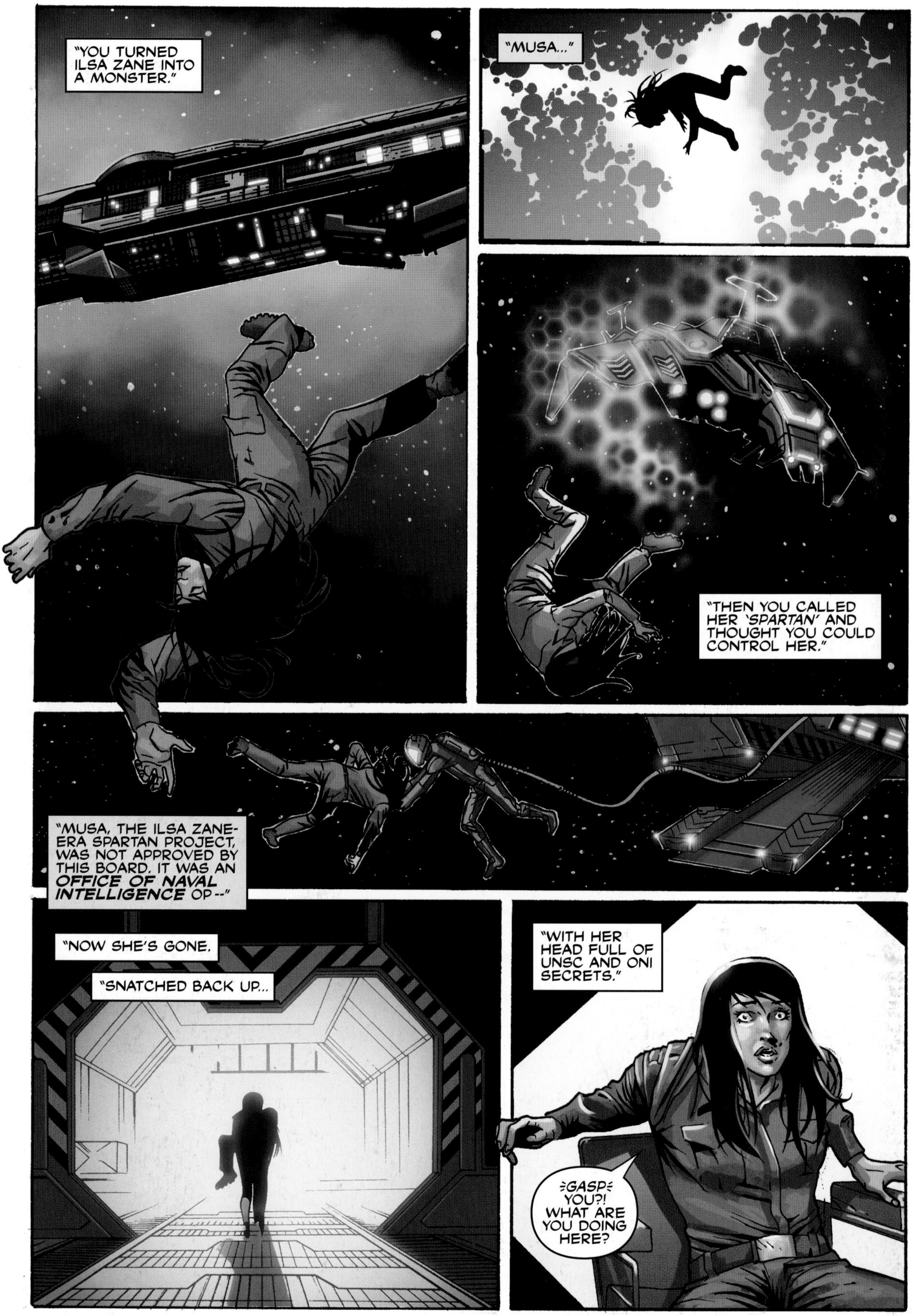
"YOU TURNED ILSA ZANE INTO A MONSTER."
"MUSA..."
"THEN YOU CALLED HER '*SPARTAN*' AND THOUGHT YOU COULD CONTROL HER."
"MUSA, THE ILSA ZANE-ERA SPARTAN PROJECT, WAS NOT APPROVED BY THIS BOARD. IT WAS AN ***OFFICE OF NAVAL INTELLIGENCE*** OP--"
"NOW SHE'S GONE.
"SNATCHED BACK UP...
"WITH HER HEAD FULL OF UNSC AND ONI SECRETS."
GASP YOU?! WHAT ARE YOU DOING HERE?

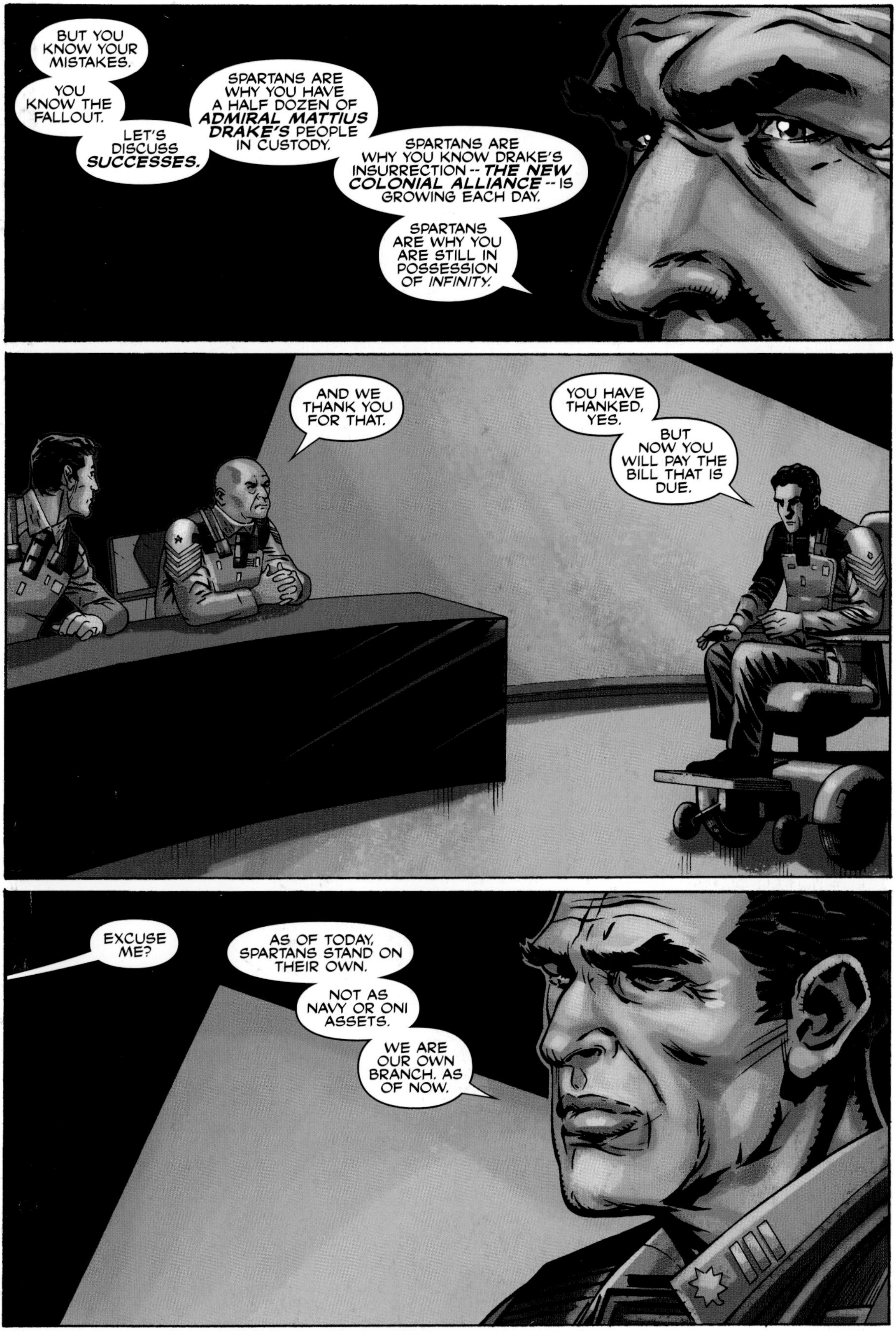
BUT YOU KNOW YOUR MISTAKES.
YOU KNOW THE FALLOUT.
LET'S DISCUSS SUCCESSES.
SPARTANS ARE WHY YOU HAVE A HALF DOZEN OF ADMIRAL MATTIUS DRAKE'S PEOPLE IN CUSTODY.
SPARTANS ARE WHY YOU KNOW DRAKE'S INSURRECTION -- THE NEW COLONIAL ALLIANCE -- IS GROWING EACH DAY.
SPARTANS ARE WHY YOU ARE STILL IN POSSESSION OF INFINITY.
AND WE THANK YOU FOR THAT.
YOU HAVE THANKED, YES.
BUT NOW YOU WILL PAY THE BILL THAT IS DUE.
EXCUSE ME?
AS OF TODAY, SPARTANS STAND ON THEIR OWN.
NOT AS NAVY OR ONI ASSETS.
WE ARE OUR OWN BRANCH. AS OF NOW.

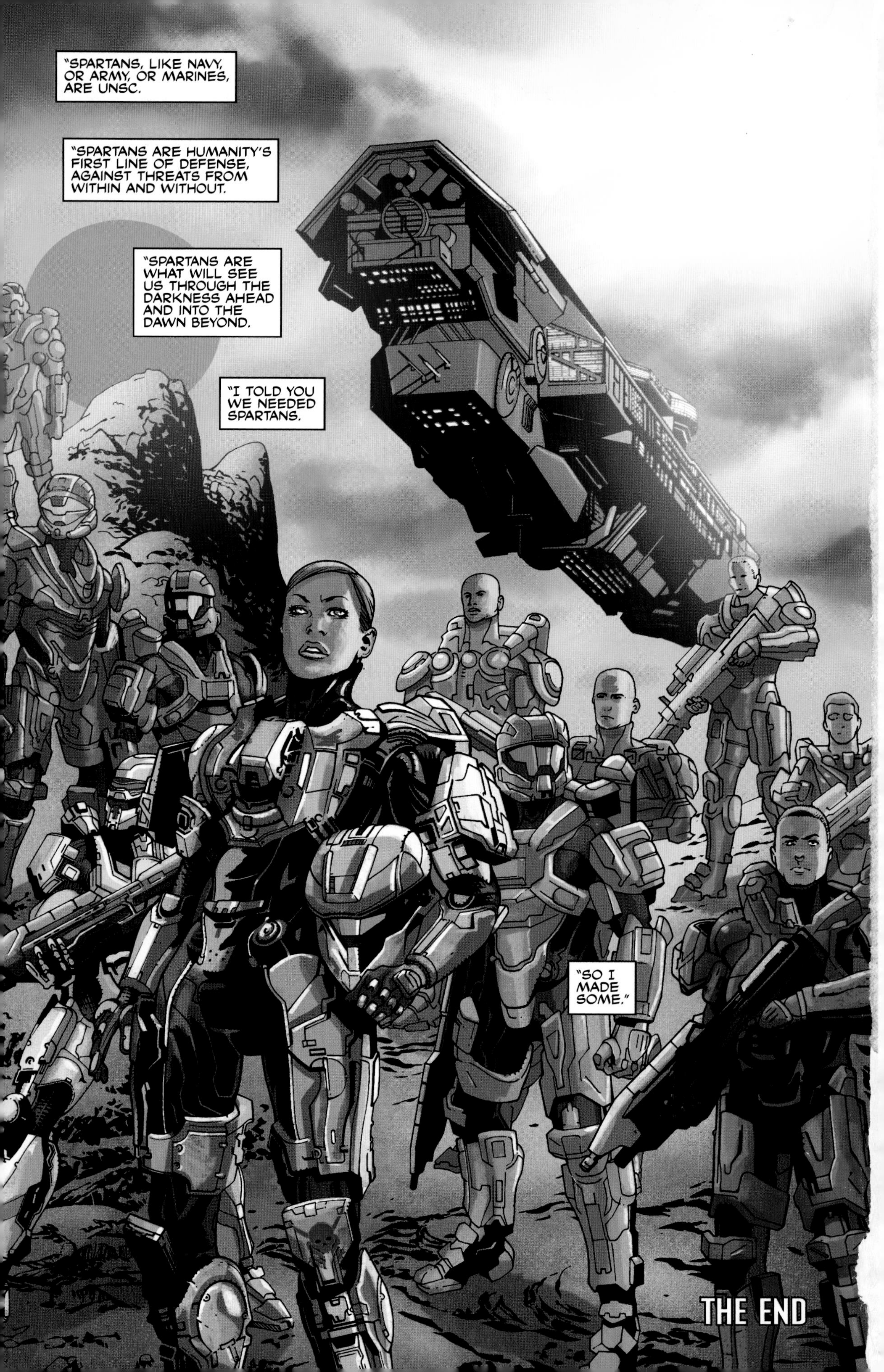
"SPARTANS, LIKE NAVY, OR ARMY, OR MARINES, ARE UNSC.
"SPARTANS ARE HUMANITY'S FIRST LINE OF DEFENSE, AGAINST THREATS FROM WITHIN AND WITHOUT.
"SPARTANS ARE WHAT WILL SEE US THROUGH THE DARKNESS AHEAD AND INTO THE DAWN BEYOND.
"I TOLD YOU WE NEEDED SPARTANS.
"SO I MADE SOME."
THE END